Mixed Troubles

Mixed Troubles

How to Play Mixed Doubles
with Your Spouse and Live to Tell About It

The Carter Brothers

ABOOKS

Alive Book Publishing

Additional copies may be ordered from the publisher for educational,
business, promotional or premium use.
For information, contact ALIVE Book Publishing at:
alivebookpublishing.com, or call (925) 837-7303

Cover and Book Design by Alex Johnson

ISBN 13: 978-1-63132-094-1

Library of Congress Control Number: 2020907366
Library of Congress Cataloging-in-Publication Data
is available upon request.

First Edition

Published in the United States of America by ALIVE Book Publishing
and ALIVE Publishing Group, imprints of Advanced Publishing LLC
3200 A Danville Blvd., Suite 204, Alamo, California 94507
alivebookpublishing.com

PRINTED IN THE UNITED STATES OF AMERICA

10 9 8 7 6 5 4 3 2 1

To Kristi
You were a driver and great coach
who provided gentle pushes along the way.
You knew this book would help others.
Thank you for your consistent dedication
in helping us complete this book.

To err is human.
To put the blame on someone else is doubles.
—Author unknown

Table of Contents

Preface

We told a friend we were thinking of writing a book to help married couples have a better experience playing tennis together. We said the title might be *For Better or For Worse: How Married Couples Can Be Happy Playing Mixed Doubles Together*. He pondered the concept for a moment, took a sip from his martini, and said, "Great idea . . . Yeah, that could be the title and then you open the book and it's only one page, and on that page it says, 'DON'T!'" That response was the confirmation that we needed to begin this work.

We are the Carter brothers (Mike, Greg, and Pat), and we are tennis players. We've lived through the drama of mixed doubles play, including sleeping on the couch from time to time. We've encountered couples exchanging heated volleys of verbal harpoons as they made their way off the court. Often the last comment heard was something like, "That's it! I'm never playing this game with you again. Never, get it?" Does that sound familiar?

Hoping to find a better way, we interviewed fellow players, talked with tennis pros, and researched relevant literature. We enlisted a professional Marriage and Family Life Counselor to provide her expertise. We believe we have found that 'better way' and are happy to have the opportunity to share it with you. Our objective, and the purpose of this book, is to give couples a game plan to help them enjoy playing tennis together, socially or in competition. We believe our story will help you win more points both on and off the court while enriching your relationship and love of the game.

Introduction

Couples play the Dating Game and the Newlywed Game. They eat, sleep, vacation, and have fun together. They work to succeed at many of the challenges life presents—buying a home, raising children, starting a business, paying for college tuitions, saving for retirement. They celebrate holidays, anniversaries, birthdays, and Valentine's Day. A husband and wife are mentally, spiritually, and emotionally connected.

Then, they attempt to play the game of mixed doubles, and often the trouble starts. Why is it that under the pressure of competition, boundaries are crossed, defense systems go up, tempers flare, and points are lost? Why is it that when a married couple steps onto the tennis court, divorce court may seem imminent?

The dynamics of singles and doubles are quite different. In a singles match, it's just you—mentally and physically—trying to overcome obstacles and find ways to score against your opponent. In a doubles match, another element enters into the equation, and that's your partner. When that partner is your spouse, it can get especially tricky. One plus one can equal a good time, or one plus one can create an emotional explosion. We'll show you how to approach the game in a way that will allow you not only to survive, but to thrive.

In the narratives that follow, we will relive our own journey through three couples that we have created to portray our story, point by point, playing in a tennis tournament (it's a little safer for us to do it this way, if you know what we mean). These characters are also an amalgamation of couples we have observed and interviewed regarding mixed doubles. We did consider drawing exclusively on our own experiences in this book; however, what we learned in our research, both on and off the court, encompassed much more than our individual experiences.

You will see how things can quickly go astray and how the same set of circumstances can be managed in a way that leads to a better experience. Recaps and a summary of key success points will underscore the most important observations. Additionally, our real-life wives weigh in after each story with their perspectives on what it is like for them playing with us and what they too have learned along the way.

You will meet Dr. Clara, a fictitious psychologist and marriage counselor with a particular interest in how couples cope under stress. She too is an amalgamation of professionals with whom we have spoken and studies we have researched. You will get to know her as she critiques and counsels couples playing in the Ambrose Woods Mixed Doubles Tennis Tournament.

We conclude this Introduction with a brief comment on how the book is organized. In Part I, we step onto the court and follow three couples as they learn to turn mixed troubles into better mixed doubles. We include a deeper dive into what is taking place beneath the surface. We also summarize highlights of our interviews with real-life couples and what they had to say about their mixed doubles experiences. Part II provides tips and strategies to improve play.

Enjoy your reading—the ball is in your court!

Part I

Stepping onto the Court
with Couples

Chapter 1

Bart and Jeanne
Round One: Stop the Madness, Please!

One evening, the three of us were on our way home with some tennis teammates. We were talking about the match we had just played, and in particular, our doubles play. The conversations went back and forth between the shots we wished we could take over, and the shots that ultimately won our lines. The chatter drifted from our match to playing mixed doubles, and then to playing mixed doubles with our wives. One of the guys remarked, "My wife and I have a rule when we play together. No matter where we play, we have to take two cars. That way we don't have to drive home together after the match."

Needless to say, there were a few chuckles and also a few head nods. Wow, separate cars. Fortunately, there is a better way. By implementing a few keys to success, which we describe in this and future chapters, you and your partner may actually enjoy your time together on the courts.

One of the keys to success is to *agree about what you hope to accomplish by playing together*. Well in advance of your match and away from the courts, couples should talk about their objectives. Do you want to win, just have fun, or both? From a relationship standpoint, what outcome would make it a success? Are you participating in a social match, or is it something more competitive? After talking with many mixed doubles partners, it seems to us that there is often a mismatch between objectives. That is a setup for a poor experience on the courts.

To illustrate the importance of having a shared objective, let's

take a look at a fictitious couple, the Wallingers. Our story is
set at the Ambrose Woods Mixed Doubles Tournament. Imagine attending a mixed doubles tournament chock-full of spouses
competing together—many for the first time. Great fun or a
powder keg ready to blow? No doubt a little of both. Let's see
what happens!

***

Nine months ago, on their 20th wedding anniversary, Bart
gave his wife, Jeanne, a new tennis racquet and signed them up
for individual lessons at the club. Neither had played much tennis since their college days, and Bart thought it would be a nice
activity for both of them. They were in good shape and in good
health. With the kids away at college, Bart figured they would
finally have some time to play.

The idea was a smashing success. Bart and Jeanne both
played more than they had expected to, and each progressed
well.

Bart played in a league and found a group of guys to play
with on a regular basis. He was a good athlete and was happy
at first with how quickly his game progressed. When he first
started, he didn't have much power on his serve and none on
his second. He was frankly embarrassed by the lollipops he was
presenting to his opponents.

"I'm not playing again until I learn to serve," he said to
Jeanne at one point. But eventually he found more power and
more consistency and soon felt more confident stepping onto the
court. He enjoyed moving up the ranks among the members of
the club as his game improved.

"How'd it go?" Jeanne would ask when he came in the door
after a match.

"I kicked his bootie!" was Bart's favorite emphatic reply—
when he won. When he lost, he mumbled about needing lessons

or more practice.

Jeanne thought it was terrific that Bart had found a sport he could enjoy and that the exercise and energy he derived from playing were great. Jeanne also enjoyed playing. A good athlete herself, she too had picked up the game quickly. She concentrated on her technique and took a number of lessons to improve her strokes. She flourished in another area—the social side of the game. She joined a women's team and also played with a morning group at their club. She met a number of women she hadn't known before and became fast friends with them. Playing at the club led to lunches out, card games, double dates with the husbands, and other social interactions. Certainly, spending time with those new friends was a welcome aspect of her new-found sport.

Bart couldn't help but notice that Jeanne was taking to tennis. He was pleased that she was enjoying the sport. "How did it go?" he would typically ask after she played.

She would respond with a self-critique: "I played pretty well," or "I wasn't really on my game today," or "We did okay, but I hit a lot of forehands into the net."

Bart would empathize and sometimes offer a tip. He found it interesting that she didn't talk about who won the match. "But who won?" he would need to ask if he wanted to know.

Perhaps the best thing about the Wallingers' new sport was the opportunity to play together. Once or twice a week, they hit together. Both got a lot out of it. Bart found that even though he was clearly the stronger player, Jeanne could rally with him and even return some of his better shots. Jeanne enjoyed the opportunity to work on her strokes, and she appreciated Bart's backing off a bit so they could extend the rallies. They practiced serving and volleying and played games they made up that were semi-competitive. They were together outdoors in the sun, being active and playing a game they enjoyed. It was fun—truly quality time.

One morning Bart read a notice in the paper about a nearby mixed doubles tournament. He was feeling good about his improving game, and he knew Jeanne was playing well. He thought it would be great to expand their tennis activity to what he considered a new level.

"Jeanne, there's a mixed doubles tournament in Bennington in a few weeks, the Ambrose Woods Mixed Doubles. I think it would be fun to enter," he said to her that evening. "It's our level and everyone is guaranteed three matches. What do you think? I hear it's a really nice facility."

"Mixed doubles—that's a man and a woman, right? Do you know anyone else who's playing?" she asked. She had to admit that the thought of playing in a tournament sounded exciting.

"No," he replied. "But I'll bet we'll know some people."

"I'll bet the Thomases will play. They love playing doubles. And the Gerringers." She paused. "We've never played together. Are you sure you want to play with me?"

"Believe me, Jeanne, there's nothing I'd like more. I think it would be fun," Bart said again. With that, they entered the tournament.

Chapter 2

Opening Night at the Ambrose Woods Tournament

The crowd was in a festive mood for the opening night bash at the Ambrose Woods Mixed Doubles Tournament. The ballroom was packed with players waiting to hear comments from Hal McIntyre, the club president, and from psychologist Dr. Clara Richardson. Dr. Clara's presence was creating a buzz. She was engaged in a study that hoped to provide insights into a question that was of great interest to many of the tournament participants: What is it about playing mixed doubles with a spouse that can cause emotions to rise so quickly?

Hal McIntyre walked across the stage to the podium. "Good evening everyone. I'm club president Hal McIntyre, and on behalf of all of us here at Ambrose Woods Country Club, I want to welcome you to the Ambrose Woods Mixed Doubles Tournament!" The crowd responded enthusiastically.

McIntyre continued, "I know that I am standing between you and cocktails, so I'll be brief." Another round of applause came from the crowd. He acknowledged the applause with a bemused smile and continued, "Very funny. This year, we are fortunate to have with us Dr. Clara Richardson. Dr. Clara is a psychologist that specializes in relationships. Over the years she has developed a focus in the area of relationships within the confines of sporting competition. She has conducted extensive research on the topic and mixed doubles is of particular interest to her. As amazing as it sounds, she has many interesting insights that can quite possibly help you leave this tournament with your marriage still intact! I'd like to welcome her to the stage."

As Dr. Clara approached the stage, the crowd applauded politely and watched her intently.

"The game of tennis seems to bring out one's base human nature quicker than other competitive sports," she began. "Now add to that the differences in the way women and men react to stress both physically and mentally. Throw in the fact that husbands' and wives' familiarity reduces the pretense for civility. The resulting situation in mixed doubles spells trouble, and the situation can become combustible quite quickly."

"There are really are no other sports where a woman and man compete together like in mixed doubles; particularly when they are wife and husband. Can you think of any? It is fascinating to me. It can lead to, let's say, interesting outcomes." Many members of the audience nodded in agreement.

She took a few steps forward. "Ladies and gentlemen, I am a psychologist. I make a good part of my living counseling married couples. And believe me, a mixed doubles tournament is fertile ground for finding new clients!" The crowd erupted with laughter.

Dr. Clara spread her papers on the podium.

"Let me tell you a short story.

"Roy Benson wakes up early and finds himself standing in front of his bathroom mirror. His salt and pepper hair is disheveled from the night's slumber. 'I can't wait until tomorrow,' he says.

'Why's that?' his wife Anne replies.

'Because, I get better looking every day!'" More laughter from the crowd.

Dr. Clara smiled and continued, "'I would agree with that,' Anne replies as she combs her hair. She is standing by the sink next to Roy's.

'That's one of the reasons I like you...always positive, and you make me feel good,' say Roy. 'What time is our match?'

'It's at 10:00 a.m. and that's only about an hour away, you

better get a move on.'

Sharing the same mirror, they can see each other's reflection. Anne is putting on her make-up and Roy is shaving.

This day involves the dynamics of mixed tennis. As Anne looks into the mirror, thoughts and worries about playing together begin to grow inside her. Roy peers into Anne's image, and his mind begins to ponder the match as well. Will we play well together? Will we win? Will we kill each other?"

Knowing chuckles came from the crowd. Dr. Clara smiled, walked out from behind the podium, and addressed the crowd, "Roy and Anne's internal anxiety meters have already moved to medium-high. They are thinking about the match and how each of them will respond to the other under the pressure of competition. Can you relate to this situation?"

The crowd responded with murmurs and nods. "You bet I can," yelled one male player. "Why do you think I'm playing with my sister this year?" More laughs came from the crowd.

"I thought so," Dr. Clara continued. "Fellow tennis players, there is an abundance of literature written on the differences between men and women. Like your tennis racquets, males and females are strung differently in emotional, mental and physical ways. It is precisely these differences, combined with the lack of pretense between a wife and husband, and the immediacy of competition that result in combustibility."

"I mentioned I need your help. You see, I need three more couples to work with, and then I will be in a position to wrap up my study on married mixed doubles. So here is my offer: For the three couples brave enough to volunteer, I will watch your matches, observe your interactions, and then meet with you after each match to discuss what I observed. I will offer tips that may help improve your experience together on the courts."

Rumbles began to reverberate from the crowd. One man objected, "Oh my god, sign up for tennis therapy with my wife? Is she kidding? Then we'll really need a psychologist!"

"Well, I think it's a great idea. I'd love to participate in something like this," his wife replied.

Bart Wallinger turned to talk to his friend, "Do you think there's a backdoor to this place? We gotta high-tail it out of here before our wives sign us up."

"Correct, Bart," his friend replied. "The first thing my wife will say is that she's always been trying to get us to take lessons together, and now's our chance. 'It will be so good for us honey.' I'm going to have to double my blood pressure medication."

Stacey Danford was talking with some of her friends as they made their way to the Ladies' Room. "You know, participating in Dr. Clara's program would be so good for Peter and me. He's always so aggressive and into winning every point. 'Come on babe pound the woman—let's win this thing'…yuck. And the advice he throws out—you'd think he was a tennis teaching professional instead of an accountant."

As the evening wore on, Dr. Clara proved to be a popular guest. Curiosity about how husbands and wives could survive mixed doubles ran deep, and stories about attempts to play together gone horribly wrong were abundant. Dr. Clara was confident she would get her three volunteers, and she was correct: The Danfords, the Brees, and, reluctantly, the Wallingers signed up.

The next day, Dr. Clara Richardson was courtside to watch the Wallingers' first match. With intentions of having her research published in an industry journal, she looked forward to observing the couples in the Ambrose Woods Mixed Doubles Tournament. She was confident that some of her strategies for dealing with stress would be helpful to the couples as they navigated the tension on the courts.

Bart and Jeanne walked out onto the court for warm-ups prior to the match. "Let's do this," Bart said to Jeanne.

Their opponents weren't married, which surprised Jeanne, but she noticed that they were smiling and joking with one another. "They seem like nice people," she said to Bart.

"Yeah. What side do you want to play?" he asked.

"I don't care," she replied. "I play both in my morning league—whatever my partner wants."

Bart already knew he wanted to play backhand. He had read enough to know that more of the important points were served to the ad court. "Okay, why don't you play forehand. You have a good forehand," Bart said. "And watch these guys while we warm up. Try to look for weaknesses."

"Does he think I'm an idiot?" she thought. But it occurred to her that it usually wasn't until well into a match that she started to really notice an opponent's weakness. And even then, she didn't necessarily change her game because of it. She began to sense that Bart really wanted to win, and she wondered what else she should be doing.

After warm-ups, Jeanne was standing behind the baseline, swinging her racquet over and over.

"What are you doing?" Bart asked.

"Oh, I think I need to take my racquet back a little farther on my forehand, and I'm having a hard time getting the timing."

"Are you crazy?" he thought. "You decide to change your stroke just before the match starts?" He was able to hold it in— for the most part. "Your forehand is fine—now's not the time to mess with it," he said, more forcefully than he'd intended. He turned and walked over to the bench.

They spun racquets, selected side and serve, and were ready to begin. Bart was keyed up, ready to play hard. As he walked onto the court, he saw Jeanne talking with the woman on the other team. He waited a minute, frustrated, then walked over to see what they were discussing.

Jeanne and her opponent had already discovered that they were both from the Southeast. They were discussing hometowns. Bart was appalled that they would get into this type of conversation right before the game, and he broke in to say,

"Ladies, we should get started."

The women stopped talking, and both gave him a quick glare. He in turn thought to himself as he turned away, "Oh jeez, I ticked them both off. Am I a jerk for being all about the match?"

Jeanne didn't say anything to him as she walked over to receive serve. She was already getting nervous because of Bart's demeanor, and his comment hadn't helped.

Things went surprisingly well for the Wallingers at the start. They were both nervous, but their play was complementary, though they didn't talk a lot. Bart was keyed up, on his game, hitting good shots and covering a lot of the net. Jeanne was playing her game, steady and deliberate. They went up 4-2, with their opponents serving. "Pivotal game seven," Bart thought. Then, Jeanne netted an easy service return, and Bart grimaced. He then proceeded to do the same. At 30-0, Jeanne netted again. She walked back behind the baseline and once again swung her racquet a number of times. "What, working on your swing again?" Bart said, with dripping sarcasm.

The moment he said it, he wished he hadn't. She looked at him, genuinely surprised—and hurt—that he had cut into her. Then, she got angry, and the flare-up was fast. "Worry about your own freaking game," she snapped. Already, they were talking to each other with a level of intensity and anger that they had rarely experienced in their 20 years of marriage. She wanted to say more, and he wanted to take it all back. But it was time for the next point. During the changeover they didn't speak.

They lost the next three games in short order.

Between sets, frustrated by losing after leading 4-2, Bart tried to get things back on track. "Okay, honey, we played well. You played well. We were up 4-2. We just need to keep playing our game," he said. "The girl's backhand is weak; let's keep hitting at her. We can beat these guys. That guy seems like he keeps hitting it at you so be ready." Jeanne could see in his body language how badly he wanted to win.

She looked at him, "I'm sorry but I'm not going to pick on Sandy. You want to win too much."

"Too much?" he snapped. "What do you think we're doing here? It's a tournament. We try to win. He's hitting at you. That's what you do in mixed doubles."

"I know, I know he's hitting at me," she said, accepting as fact what she had hoped was just her imagination. She was upset. "I don't know why. Isn't this supposed to be fun for everyone?"

"Don't worry, honey. Let's just get them this set. We can beat these freakin' jerks."

That was it. Jeanne stifled a sob and shot back, "Look, I just want to play a good match and hit some good shots. You can do what you want. This competitiveness is too much for me. And this is the last time I'm playing with you." She picked up her racquet and headed to the court. The second set started poorly, and, as the losses mounted, both of them couldn't wait to get off the court.

Chapter 3

Courtside Coaching:
Dr. Clara Works with the Wallingers
The Authors Offer a Deeper Look

On opening night, Bart and Jeanne were the last of the three couples to sign up to work with Dr. Clara during the tournament. When they signed up, Dr. Clara was glad to have them. Now, she wasn't so sure. A half hour after the match, Dr. Clara went looking for Bart and Jeanne for their post-match discussion. She found them at a table in the far corner of the lounge.

"Guys, that was ugly out there. What do you think happened?" Dr. Clara asked.

Jeanne was still hurting. "This isn't for me. Bart turned into a rude, self-centered you-know-what that only cared about winning and didn't care at all about me," she said.

Bart just sat there, staring at the ground. After a moment of awkward silence, Dr. Clara said, "I watched your interactions closely and overheard some of your comments. It seems to me you two had different objectives for this match. Bart, you clearly wanted to win. And Jeanne, you didn't seem to share that same drive. You were looking at the match differently, and the pressure of the tournament caused each of you to become very frustrated with each other's behavior. Bart, I have to say, you have some things to work out. You need to let go of the need to control. When you told Jeanne not to change her stroke, you were treating her as a subordinate. You also seemed overly critical. You need to concentrate on your own game. Being critical of your partner's game can devolve into a nasty, negative mindset on the court. And I think you need to find some tools to deal with your anger. It seemed to flare up out there."

Dr. Clara wasn't done yet. She turned to Jeanne, "Jeanne, I know it's hard, but you should at least consider where Bart is coming from. Doing so will make his comments more understandable and hopefully a little less hurtful. Is it really that out of line for Bart to want to win? This is a tennis tournament after all. Most importantly, for both of you, I think you would benefit from having a discussion a day or two before your next match where you talk about what you hope to accomplish on the court. Is it to win at all costs? Is it to have fun playing together? I think you'll find that this type of discussion can be very helpful."

***

Recap

Let's leave Bart and Jeanne's saga for a moment and take a more analytical look at what happened in their first match.

Bart and Jeanne had different objectives. They went into the match with a different focus. Bart clearly wanted to win, and Jeanne didn't have the same drive. Bart was focused on beating the competition. He took an adversarial position in regard to the other team. Jeanne was focused on the social aspects of the game. She took a joining position, not opposing the other team.

A tournament increases pressure, and playing doubles increases the pressure even more. Pressure heightens concerns over performance and, especially, how one's performance appears to others. The pressure transfers these concerns more quickly and more directly to one's self-esteem. Because of this, bad behavior and defensiveness can spill out quickly.

Jeanne has some items to think about. Mixed doubles players need to consider their partner's perspective. To an extent, Jeanne views the tournament as a social event. She does not seem to have considered that winning the match may be a reasonable objective. Based on her view of the event, Bart's actions are, of course, completely inconsistent with appropriate behavior. If she were to understand Bart's motivations for the match, she might interpret Bart's comments in a way that is less hurtful to her.

Bart needs to work on a few things as well. Telling someone what to do (or what not to do) takes away the enjoyment of the game and creates defensiveness. Defensiveness in turn increases mistakes and a breakdown in communication. Bart must learn to refrain from trying to assert control and instead communicate in a way that preserves Jeanne's dignity.

He also should be aware of thinking that is critical of others. Looking for a weakness in an opponent is a sound strategy, but it can lead to a critical outlook, including looking for weaker spots in a partner. It can foster a critical attitude toward everyone.

Furthermore, Bart's use of sarcasm is particularly concerning, as it is often a sign of hidden hostility in a relationship. While an important aspect of tennis strategy is to exploit the opponent's weakness, Bart needs to maintain the mental awareness to ensure that this critical mindset does not extend to other aspects of the game, especially to his partner. Remember: Attitudes are contagious.

Anger is another issue for Bart. Anger and nerves dissolve concentration and performance. Bart's demeanor and body language communicate disapproval, disappointment, and disrespect toward his wife. All of these are manifestations of anger. The couple couldn't wait to end the game, which was a way to stop the tension and anger. There was no conflict resolution while on the court.

This couple would benefit from better communication regarding the larger picture of their goals. A great step would be to discuss the purpose of the match, why they are playing together, and what they hope to accomplish.

Bart and Jeanne's experience in this match underscores one of the keys to success: Again, couples should discuss their objectives for the match beforehand. Is the objective to win, or to have fun together? Is it some combination of both? Under the pressure of competition, with spectators watching and pride on the line, it is critical for couples to keep perspective on what they are hoping to accomplish together on the courts. A strong sense of that objective is required, as it is easily lost when the game is on.

Keys to Success
- *Talk before the match.*
- *Agree on what you hope to accomplish in the match.*
- *Understand your partner's motivations.*
- *Come up with the basics of your strategy, such as who plays where.*

Chapter 4

Bart and Jeanne
Round Two: Just You and Me

Before we rejoin Bart and Jeanne for their next match, what else besides a pre-match discussion of objectives can help avoid disaster on the court?

Couples should try to gain perspective on why they play tennis in the first place. *Understanding your partner's motivation for the match* is another key to success in mixed doubles. It is a bit unreasonable to expect a social player who enjoys being outdoors and seeing friends to suddenly take on a menacing, I'm-going-to-deliver-a-beat-down attitude.

Let's get back to Bart and Jeanne and see how the idea of understanding your partner's motivations plays a role in their story.

***

After their first match, the ride home for Bart and Jeanne began with stone cold silence on the outside and churning emotions on the inside. Jeanne was understandably upset and felt let down by her partner. Bart finally summoned the courage to break the ice and get what was coming his way.

"Jeanne, that was awful out there. And I don't mean the tennis," he said.

"Yes, it was. You humiliated me and made me feel worthless," she shot back.

"I know. I'm sorry. I just wanted to win, and I lost control," he said contritely.

They drove in silence for a while longer, both letting the tension level dissipate. Jeanne restarted the conversation, "Bart, I think Dr. Clara brought up some good ideas for us after the match. She watched us closely, and she saw that I was upset. I'm willing to play in the next match with you if we try some of the things she mentioned. Let's talk about why we are playing together in the first place. Dr. Clara said we have different motivations. I know how badly you want to win—I see that now—and I guess I can understand that. For me, the most important thing is enjoying the event—meeting new people and getting some exercise. I want to play well and feel good about my game. That's what I care about. That's winning to me."

"Well, I do want to win," replied Bart. "But I can see that it's not worth it to win if we hurt each other in the process. I'm not sure I can get out there with a mindset of just trying to enjoy the tournament, the people and all of that. But I should be able to stay positive and supportive and keep my emotions in check."

"Okay," said Jeanne. "Dr. Clara said we should agree on what we are trying to accomplish. Let's agree that we are going to be supportive and enjoy the match while we try to win."

"Done," said Bart. "She also suggested that we discuss match strategy in advance so that we don't have the extra tension of figuring it out on the fly. I thought you hit your forehand well. And, to be honest, all the books on strategy say the stronger player should take the ad side, so let's commit to that."

"Okay," Jeanne replied. "What about coming to the net? I'm comfortable coming in. Let's start off a little more aggressive and see how it goes."

"Great," said Bart. "And let's not be afraid to talk during points. Let's call it, and if you want me to move left or right, just tell me."

On the day of their second match, Bart and Jeanne ran into Dr. Clara outside the facility. Jeanne had told Dr. Clara that she and Bart were going to concentrate more on staying positive and having fun. Apparently, though, when they walked onto the court for the beginning of their second match, they found it was easier said than done.

For Bart, the competitive juices began flowing immediately, and it occurred to him that maybe he was right after all: The most important thing was to win. He looked at Jeanne, thought about their conversation, and realized he was at the moment of truth. Maybe she was right. Maybe it was about having fun and just enjoying the event. Could they both be right? Under the mounting pressure, he was confused. As the match started, he resolved to try his best to win and at the same time, to be supportive, positive, and pleasant in his exchanges with Jeanne.

As Jeanne walked onto the court, she was also thinking about their conversation. "Okay," she thought. "I'm going to try to play my best, and I'm going to try to help us win. And if Bart does lose control of his emotions, at least I know it's just because he wants to win." But she too found that it wasn't easy. She was immediately more nervous than usual, and she found it uncomfortable to be so focused on defeating another team.

The play was tense. Jeanne and Bart's interaction was awkward. When Bart missed an easy overhead, he stomped his foot in disgust and swore under his breath. He immediately questioned himself—was his reaction overblown? Jeanne resisted the urge to give him a glare and instead offered a meek, "It's okay, you'll get the next one." When Jeanne misplayed balls, Bart tamped down his frustration, told himself it was only a game, and offered a quick, if insincere, "Don't worry about it."

With the added burden of controlling their emotions, both Bart and Jeanne found it more difficult to focus on their tennis. They lost the first set 6-3.

At the crossover, Jeanne, acutely aware of Bart's desire to win, thought to herself, "This is it for me. I don't really like competing, and I'm letting Bart down. I am just really uncomfortable with the pressure of all of this."

She said to Bart, "Well, we didn't win the set, but we did win a few games. I know I cost us some important points. I'm sorry I'm not playing well." She looked dejected.

Bart had never before seen her look sad on the court. She was always smiling and having fun. He realized he had caused it. He was heartsick. His demeanor changed. "Oh, honey," he said. "Don't worry about that. You're playing fine. And remember what we talked about; we're out here to have fun together and enjoy all of this." He stroked her hair. "Come on, let's go have fun this second set. That's all."

Out they went. Words of encouragement between the two were more frequent. Though the exchanges still felt forced and over the top, both appreciated each other's effort. Soon, they both began to embrace their new way of playing. They discovered that winning the relationship game—staying positive even while being pounded by their opponents—was a victory that held some importance.

As play wore on, they got in sync with their new relationship dynamics on the court and began to focus more on their tennis. Their attitudes were positive and healthy. They played better. They dug themselves a hole early in the second set, down 1-4, but fought back to tie things up at 6-6.

Bart was excited. He said to himself, "Wow, we're in this thing! We have a chance to win. Tiebreaker now—I have to step it up." He looked over at Jeanne, "You're playing great. Keep it up!"

The pressure of the tiebreaker was building in Jeanne, and the mindset of being positive and enjoying the match was pushed aside by the tension of the moment. She heard the old desire to win in Bart's comment, which only added to the pressure.

Bart and Jeanne won the first two points of the tiebreaker, but their opponents won the next two. On point five, Jeanne dumped an easy forehand into the net. Bart implored her to keep trying, but it was clear that he was once again focused only on winning. Jeanne understood why, but under the pressure of the match, she snapped back, "There you go again—it's all about winning. Don't you think I'm trying?"

Instead of replying, Bart grimaced. "I don't need a break-down now while we are still in this," he thought. He kept it in-side.

The serve came to Bart, and he returned it cross-court to the server, who played the ball back to him. Bart tried a shot down the alley but pulled it wide for an unforced error. He grabbed the handle of his racquet with both hands, squeezed it as if he were wringing a chicken's neck, and muttered a number of ex-pletives under his breath in obvious disgust.

"Oh, great," Jeanne said. "That's how you try to just have fun out here. I don't know if you can." They dropped the tiebreaker and lost the match in straight sets.

Chapter 5

Dr. Clara Works with the Wallingers
The Authors Offer a Deeper Look

At their post-match debrief, Dr. Clara started on the bright side. "You two started off in the right direction," she began. "Your discussion prior to the match carried over to the court, at least at the beginning. It isn't easy to change your objective to something other than wanting to win. It takes work and persistence. It looked like you were trying to focus on getting along while at the same time still trying to do all you could do to win. It's a lot. And, it is especially difficult given the pressure of competition and in front of so many people." She paused. "I'm going to suggest something that may sound strange. I want you to go out and practice being supportive. Go hit some balls, and lay it on thick. It will feel awkward and insincere. That's okay. It will help you open up to a different mind-set."

***

Recap

Jeanne and Bart had discussed, prior to the match, what they hoped to accomplish. However, they chose a goal that was not realistic given where they are as a couple and under the pressures of a tournament. They agreed that having fun together and enjoying the event is important, and so is winning. The dual goal is just too big at this stage. If winning is the dominant goal, it will be very difficult to be supportive and to enjoy the game when playing a competitive match. It is not impossible but doing so would be a huge step given their disastrous playing relationship in the first match.

Changing behavior is not easy. Their new objective required different behavior, and both Bart and Jeanne found that changing behavior was not so simple. Jeanne found that ramping up her desire to win and changing the focus of the tennis was not easy. When the match started, and the adrenaline started to flow, Bart reverted to his conviction that winning is paramount. It was only when he sees that he had taken all of the joy out of the game for his wife—a game she loves—that he finds the resolve to commit to the behaviors that put enjoyment of the match above winning.

Bart and Jeanne failed because they asked too much of themselves too soon. Jeanne made an honest effort to focus more on winning and to be more accepting of Bart's desire to win. Bart wanted to win, and he put up a front of being supportive and positive. He may even have convinced himself, but as soon as the pressure built, he found that it was not possible to maintain the charade.

When victory seemed to be at hand, Jeanne also abandoned the idea of focusing on enjoying the match and instead focused on winning. She is not comfortable with this motivation. The pressure and her nerves immediately took a toll.

Bart and Jeanne need to truly commit to the objective of enjoying the time together. The positive, supportive behavior required is not easy for either of them. Only by fully committing to making the changes will Jeanne and Bart be able to move their tennis relationship to a better place. As they continue to work on managing their attitudinal priorities, the outward changes will exhibit themselves.

As the saying goes, "practice makes perfect"—in tennis as well as in social skills. Couples who want to get along well on the court should practice doing so. Practicing being positive and supportive, as strange as it sounds, can be helpful. Try going out and just hitting with your spouse, and while you are at it, go over the top with the support and compliments. You may be surprised how it translates in matches.

Keys to Success
- *Recognize that changing behavior isn't easy, especially in the heat of competition.*
- *Avoid drifting into a critical attitude.*
- *Improving social skills requires practice.*

Chapter 6

Bart and Jeanne
Round Three: Will They Survive?

O ur brave couple has had a rough go of it in their first two matches together. In addition to the first three keys to success, they have also learned that changing behavior is not easy. Jeanne in particular seems to recognize that it takes effort. Let's see what transpires in their next match.

***

In the days prior to their third match, neither Bart nor Jeanne was especially excited to play. Bart knew they had no chance to move on in the tournament, and Jeanne's experiences in the first two matches were so bad that she was reluctant to play again with Bart.

"Look, Bart, let's just go out and have fun. Dr. Clara suggested that we take it one step at a time and that we should focus on being supportive of one another as a couple. She told us it wouldn't be easy—that changing behavior is very difficult. She said we need to really commit. Winning the match may come from that, or it may not. Promise you won't go all competitive on me. We're out of it, so winning doesn't matter."

Bart pursed his lips. "Okay, I know," he said. "We're out of it, so it doesn't really matter." To himself, he resolved to just work on his game during the match.

"You know, Bart, the best time I've had playing with you was in the second set of the last match when we were both being positive, as Dr. Clara suggested," Jeanne said.

"I agree. I was thinking that myself. I thought we were out of the match, and you looked sad to be out there. At that point I had a lot of motivation to be positive. I tell you what: I'm going to be positive and supportive no matter what is going on, and let's see what happens," Bart said.

"I'll tell you what," Jeanne replied. "Let's go out and hit the ball together, and practice being supportive."

"Practice being supportive? You're kidding, right?" said Bart.

"Dr. Clara said practicing behaviors is one of the best ways to make them genuine. It was her only suggestion this time. So, deal or no deal?"

Bart chuckled. "Okay, honey. It seems crazy, but what the heck."

Off they went to the practice courts. They found that making supportive comments was at first awkward and difficult. It certainly seemed forced. After a while, though, they both noticed that they liked receiving the support, even when they knew it was not particularly sincere.

When Bart crushed one at her, Jeanne commented, "Hey, Hercules, nice shot."

"Where did that come from?" Bart said playfully when Jeanne hit an especially good shot.

They began to get used to giving the support. What was awkward began to feel more natural. All in all, practicing being supportive and positive was a bit strange, but they did enjoy the exercise.

The time for the third match finally arrived and Dr. Clara dutifully took her place courtside. During the first set, both Bart and Jeanne found it easy to be positive and supportive. The pressure was off since they had no chance of advancing, and they were holding their own against the other team.

"You're playing really great," Bart said to Jeanne.

"Let's just keep playing well and having fun out here,"

Jeanne replied with enthusiasm.

As the set wore on, Bart noticed that the man on the other side tended to poach on some of Jeanne's forehands. He was going to suggest to Jeanne that she try a shot down the alley, but instead, not wanting to appear too controlling, just said, "Jeanne, that guy is poaching on you."

"I know," she said.

"Well, you have a good forehand. Maybe you should try to keep him at home and hit one down the line. Who cares anyway?"

"You know that's a difficult shot for me," Jeanne replied.

Bart turned and walked away. "Oh, brother," he thought. "Why bother. It'll just turn into an argument. She doesn't care at all about winning."

Their body language didn't look good. In the stands, Dr. Clara thought, "Uh-oh. Here we go again."

Sure enough, on the next point, the opponent poached again on Jeanne. Bart bit his lip, gave Jeanne an encouraging smile, and got in position for the next point.

"Whatever," she thought. "This isn't much fun but at least I know the lunch spread is great…Since we're trying to have fun, though, and we're out of it anyway, maybe I'll try some tougher shots."

She hit her next serve-return down the alley for a winner! After an extended moment of remaining perfectly still, Bart swiveled at the hips, looked at Jeanne playfully, and said, "Where did that come from?" He spun his racquet in his hands, and strutted back to the baseline, whistling. Jeanne smiled and laughed. Bart laughed too and said, "Great shot, honey!"

Bart crushed his serve-return, but well deep.

"Yo, Hercules, nice rip," Jeanne said. Bart laughed.

For the remainder of the match, they joked and played with one another. The tension had left their game, and their tennis improved. They won some games and lost some games. But they hardly noticed because they were having fun. At the crossover, they were almost giddy. "Now this," Bart said, "is fun!"

Jeanne agreed, and her smile was back.

"I've been having fun the last few games," said Bart. "For the first time I think we can have a blast and, what the heck, maybe play well while we're at it."

And that they did. They concentrated on hitting good shots, and after each and every point—good and bad—their comments to one another had the same underlying message: "We have something special, and that's what is most important."

They split the first two sets and won the third 6-2. They didn't advance because of their losses in the first two matches, but it seemed they had advanced in a different way.

Dr. Clara sat with the Wallingers, this time at the club's bar with a round of drinks. "Well," she started, "I'll be honest. I wasn't sure you were going to be able to pull it together. In the end though the effort you made to practice being supportive and positive saved the day."

Bart and Jeanne nodded their heads in agreement.

Dr. Clara continued, "At one point during the match you both finally gave up the goal of winning. In the vacuum that ensued, the opportunity for supportive, playful interaction presented itself. Your game plan of being supportive, even in a forced manner, evolved to the realization that the fun, unconditional support that makes you a loving couple was, in fact, a better plan. Having practiced new behaviors, you were able to put it all together."

Keys to Success
- *Practicing being supportive and positive can make the difference in staying that way during competition.*
- *Committing to a singular objective is not easy to do.*
- *Breakthroughs happen.*

Chapter 7

A Woman's Perspective: Mary Carter

Communication is key to working and playing together, but not just during the match. In their first match, it would have been fruitful for Bart and Jeanne to learn a little about each other's objectives before entering the court. In addition, basic strategy, such as deciding which side each will play, should not be a court decision, but one discussed before the match.

Acceptance is also another important aspect of mixed doubles. It is essential in a marriage, and it is equally as important on the court. Bart is fully aware that off the court Jeanne is a social person and loves making connections with anyone in her path. Guess what? She is the same person at any venue. I can identify with Jeanne's love for connecting with people. I am definitely guilty of asking personal questions to my opponents. It humanizes the game. This certainly does not mean, however, that I am less interested in winning or playing my best.

One of the trickiest aspects for me when playing as a couple is separating personal attacks from helpful encouragement. I find it is sometimes difficult to leave my ego and sensitivities at the door, and to take constructive criticism (especially from my husband). There may be deep-seated issues that can surface with even the fewest words. A mixed doubles couple must decide affirmatively that they indeed can treat one another with the same respect on the court as they would any other partner.

Any athlete, amateur or professional, knows his or her own capabilities as well as shortcomings. It is condescending to try to boost a partner with a compliment of which she or he is not worthy. There is no value in doing this. It only creates more tension and disrespect. On occasions, while playing mixed doubles with my husband, he will respond to my error with, "Nice try." Really? Nice try? Quite frankly, I would rather he said, "That shot sucked." I'm all for being positive and supportive—it is critical—but it needs to be honest and appropriate. Truth be told, giving undeserved compliments can create negativity on the court. Saying nothing is probably your best bet, unless it really was a nice try even though it failed.

Speaking of remarks, sometimes a gesture or facial expression is worth a thousand words and can trigger an adverse effect. Now and then my husband will make a disgusted face after we lose a point, especially when the error is mine. Okay, that's got to go. Even though no one else may see the pouty face, it conveys a sense of disappointment. Nothing rattles my bones like a partner who gives me a feeling of worthlessness. It creates a downward spiral.

Another issue that couples may encounter is an imbalance in effort—either too much or a lack thereof. I do not attend many clinics or team practices, so my preparation for mixed doubles matches is not always stellar. When my partner has put forth more work ahead of time, and I have not, there is a feeling of guilt when I make a misplay or a positioning error. Again, understanding a partner's commitment to the game can ease the court tension.

I believe that if a couple begins a match with the mindset of, "We are a team, and although we think differently, we do so with respect," there is a chance for success. Understanding, acceptance, and communication are all needed for a good on-court relationship.

Chapter 8

Peter and Stacey
Round One: Lace 'em Up

A nother tennis-playing couple we Carter brothers would like to introduce is the Daytons. Here's their story.

***

Peter Dayton was vacationing in Scottsdale, Arizona, a trip he made annually with his sister and parents. They stayed somewhere different each year and this year decided to stay at the Vistas, a new golf and tennis resort. Peter was a 38-year-old structural engineer who had never married and lived in Glendale, California. His parents lived in Bend, Oregon, and came down to Scottsdale to visit with their children, play golf and tennis, and catch up on their busy lives.

Three days into their vacation, after going through four sleeves of golf balls and then playing two horrific rounds, Peter decided he would try tennis again. He had excelled at the game as a youngster although he had never taken it too seriously.

Peter signed up for a 9 a.m. intermediate-level tennis clinic given by the teaching pro. He was up early in anticipation of the clinic and headed down to the tennis facility to grab a cup of coffee at the Courtside Café. Peter was 6'2", handsome, well-built, and an impeccable dresser. He looked sharp in his crisp tennis whites as he arrived at the pro shop. The three other clinic participants had also arrived and were waiting for direction. They were greeted by Sammy Sanford, a 62-year-old sun-dried veteran of the game who really knew his stuff. The four were assigned to court #4 where they introduced themselves and engaged in stretching exercises. They were paired up on opposite sides of the net and were instructed to begin hitting soft shots no deeper than the service box.

Across the net from Peter were Mr. and Mrs. Kelley, retired residents of Scottsdale who often signed up for clinics with Sammy Sanford, their favorite teaching pro. On Peter's side of the net was 37-year-old Stacey, who had come to Arizona from Virginia seeking sunshine and a break from her fast-paced career as a marketing director for an electronics company.

Stacey was 5'10", competitive, as attractive as she was athletic, and topped off with a bubbly personality. She had played tennis in high school but switched to volleyball, eventually playing volleyball at an East Coast College, where she also captained the women's track team.

As the clinic got under way, Sammy barked instructions from the sidelines and kept things lively with different drills. He complimented them often saying, "You guys are making me look good!" As the instruction continued, Peter admired the way Stacey hit her ground strokes and her effortless way of moving about the court. The clinic concluded an hour later with complimentary refreshments on the tennis observation deck. Peter approached Stacey as she was sipping her iced tea and praised her on her game.

She blushed and returned the compliment. Peter ordered a Bloody Mary, and the two sipped their beverages and chatted for an hour. The conversation came effortlessly, as if they had known each other for years. Peter was totally smitten, and, not seeing a wedding band on her finger, got up the nerve to ask Stacey if she was married.

She replied, "I was, but I've been divorced for seven years."

Peter thought to himself, "Green light!" and asked Stacey out to dinner that evening. The two saw each other three times over the next couple of days. A coast-to-coast romance ensued, and after a year, the two found themselves exchanging wedding vows. Stacey relocated to Peter's home in Glendale and was fortunate to keep her marketing job with the company's West Coast branch.

Although the two had never played tennis together competitively, after their marriage they played many times socially and really enjoyed playing together. They decided to join the Court Time Tennis Club, located near their home. One day, the club pro mentioned an upcoming mixed doubles tournament called the Ambrose. The pro told them that others from the club had already signed up and suggested that they enter too.

The other teams from their club were made up of mainly single guys and gals, although there was one other married couple. The teams prepared by practicing once during the week and once on weekends, which was a great opportunity to meet people and get a feel for the level of play. The first couple of practices were quite social, culminating with adult beverages. Given that Peter was just as competitive as Stacey yet not the accomplished player she was, he thought he had better sign them up for a series of lessons being given by Oscar Owens, a member of the teaching staff. They were able to get in a few sessions before the opening of the tournament. As a final tune-up, they scheduled a practice match with another team from the club.

They arrived 15 minutes early for their 1 p.m. practice match. The sun shone brightly and almost directly overhead.

"I am nervous but super excited about this match," said Stacey as they warmed up. Their much younger opponents stepped onto the court, introduced themselves, and, after a short warm-up, the match began.

After the first couple of games, Peter and Stacey were down 0-2, prompting Peter to exclaim, "This is a lousy start! We can't get anything by these two."

Stacey replied, "Don't get discouraged. Let's figure out a way to get a couple games." It proved to be easier said than done; three games later the score was 0-5 with the momentum clearly continuing for the opponents. The first set ended 1-6, with Peter and Stacey salvaging only the sixth game.

"Let's try to put into play what we learned in our lessons," said Stacey during the changeover.

"I have been. I'm not sure what you've been doing," replied Peter sharply.

"I've been trying to clean up your messes," Stacey responded as she glared at him and walked away.

The second set got under way much in the same fashion as the first, with the speedy opponents grabbing the first two games. Stacey held serve, and the score was 1-2. At love-forty in the fourth game, Peter attempted an overhead shot that barely grazed the frame of his racquet and came to rest in the parking lot.

"Oh, that was nice," said Stacey.

"The sun sucks. I can't see a damn thing," Peter groused.

"You should have thought about bringing your sunglasses instead of watching that football game until two minutes before we had to leave," said Stacey. The second set ended and so did the match, with the opponents winning 1-6 and 3-6.

As they left the court Peter said sarcastically, "Now wasn't that fun?" The ride home was quiet.

The following week the couple skipped the team practice, so they could get in two more private lessons before the first match of the Ambrose Tournament.

Tuesday night, while waiting for the instructor to arrive, Peter said, "Hey, darling, I know that first match didn't go too well for us. We are both competitive and want to do well, but I don't think we have the skills yet to do so. Let's pay attention, work hard at these lessons, and I know good things will happen for us—like winning!"

"Excuse me, Peter, did you say you didn't think 'we' have

the skills yet to do so, or did you mean 'you'?" was Stacey's response.

"I meant me," Peter replied sheepishly.

"Okay, I'm on board with that. I'd really like to win," Stacey said.

The lesson consisted of forehand, backhand, and volley drills. After a lengthy volley demonstration by the instructor, Peter failed miserably to replicate the shot, prompting Stacey to comment, "Hello? Weren't you listening?" The dig was not taken well. Apparently, the two couldn't help but heckle one another.

Thursday's lesson was to cover serving and strategy, two areas where they were both lacking. Over the next 90 minutes, each had good and not so good shots. As the lesson ended, they also both felt as if they had learned techniques that would benefit them, and they began looking forward to the tournament.

For the first match at the Ambrose Tournament, Peter and Stacey had their game faces on before they got out of the parking lot. Dr. Clara was courtside to observe their interaction.

The other team was already on the court warming up for the 2 p.m. contest. Introductions concluded. The home team won the coin toss and elected to serve.

As they were warming up, Peter asked Stacey, "Are you ready to kick some 45-year-old butt and get a victory?"

"Way ready," replied Stacey.

The match started with the first serve kicking past Peter for an ace. The next serve to the ad side was a body shot that caromed off Stacey's knee into the net. The following two points went the way of the home team as they held serve. Peter struggled through his service game but, with a couple of unforced errors on the other side of the net, was able to hold. However, three games later, the opponents were up 4-1 and had gained the upper hand, due in large part to Peter's sloppy play.

On the changeover, a frustrated Peter asked Stacey why she wasn't being more aggressive and why she was hanging back on the base line. "You need to get to the net to win points, not hang back like a chicken," he said.

"Well, if you would quit hitting those watermelons to the net person, I would come up, but I'm tired of being a target. Why don't you hit it like a man?"

Furious with each other, they walked back onto the court to start the sixth game. With adrenaline pumping, Peter powered through his service game to bring the score to 4-2. The crafty opponents, now throwing in spin and drop shots, held easily to go up 5-2. The exchange of verbal venom had unnerved Stacey as she proceeded to double fault twice to lose the first set 6-2.

Between sets the couple had a spirited discussion about staying positive and out of each other's face. They agreed the second set would be different. They didn't know how different.

The second set began on a positive note, breaking their opponent for a 0-1 lead. Peter held serve with deep penetrating ground strokes and some sneaky poaching by Stacey. Peter was fired up and felt as if things were starting to go in their direction. Down 0-2, the opponents began showing why they did so well in last year's tournament. Over the next four games Peter and Stacey won only six points and were now behind 4-2.

The seventh game started, and Peter was beginning to get desperate. From the net Stacey turned and sprinted after a deep lob shot that she couldn't catch up to. The ball was clearly in but was called out by Peter.

"That ball wasn't out," she said to Peter.

"I know it wasn't—just keep quiet and play," he growled. Stacey was stunned at the way Peter talked to her, and that he would cheat in order to win. Her game totally fell apart. The set ended 6-2. The players shook hands and left the court.

Stacey looked at Peter with tears in her eyes. "Listen to me, you jerk," she began. "I'm just as competitive as you are, but you're too competitive for your own good. You embarrassed me today—made me feel totally inadequate. I thought we could keep this fun and enjoyable, but it's become obvious you can't. It really hurts me when you shake your head in disgust or make your scathing comments. Don't you think I'm trying to do my best out there? Well, I am! I love you, and our off-court relationship is much more important to me than these stressful matches! So what I'm saying to you, Peter, is: Get yourself another partner! I quit!"

Chapter 9

Courtside Coaching: Strung Too Tight
The Authors Offer a Deeper Look

"Wow... time out, time out," Dr. Clara said as their de-brief began. "What happened out there?"

"Dr. Clara, it's way too stressful for me playing like this. I understand that I'm competitive and like to win. However, it's not worth the mental strain. I feel this is going to fester and may carry-on off the court," said Stacey angrily.

"Why can't you just forget about it when the match is over?" Peter asked.

"Listen, Rambo, I can't just forget about it. If we don't discuss it, nothing changes," replied Stacey.

Dr. Clara jumped in, "Let's pause here for a moment, guys. One of the things you both need to learn, especially you, Peter, is the importance of knowing when to be competitive and when to back off."

"I'm not that competitive. I just put a high value on wining," Peter quipped.

"At what cost...bad line calls?" Stacey inquired.

"You two are both very competitive. You both want to win. However, in attempting to mow down your opponents, you mow down each other! It is stressful for couples to feel as if they always have to be on their game and competitive. The thought of having to compete well every time you step onto the court can become burdensome. This tournament is meaningful, I know, but in the big scheme of things, it isn't overly important. Maybe try to take it down a notch and use these times to keep it light and have fun, like when playing in a social match or event with friends at your club," Dr. Clara said.

"Peter, all I know is that you're going to have to somehow prove to me that your on-court behavior has changed before I ever get onto the court with you again," Stacey said.

***

Recap

Sarcasm with a dig is not good in a marriage. Stacey had said to Peter, "Why don't you hit like a man?" Wow! What a blow to a guy's ego. Scathing comments like that, and humiliating body language, are problematic, to put it mildly.

Peter isn't much better. He tells Stacey what she "should" do – taking the word "should" to an extreme. Actually, do any of us have the right to tell another adult what they should be doing? Do you really have the right to tell another player what they should be doing? Try going for one week without telling your spouse what they should do. It is a difficult exercise but can be insightful.

A scenario where you would want to back off from expectations of your partner is when playing an opponent with clearly superior skills. This is literally a no-win situation, and not a time to press yourself or a less skilled partner.

Peter showed he will do anything to win—even cheat! Does this reveal Peter's underlying character? Does Stacey really know this person? Wow again. The flow of testosterone and adrenaline can make people behave in ways different than they would in other situations. Peter needs to take a deep breath from time to time and remind himself that he is playing a game where sportsmanship and honesty are more important than winning and losing.

In our observations and research with many couples we have found that men and women think differently in the following ways:

In the heat of the moment, men often think they are not really being critical when they get pumped up and make scathing comments they do not actually mean.

Sometimes women think their man really feels that way underneath and that the pressure just releases the scathing comments he truly believes. Women may then question their partners' character and true feelings, creating insecurity in the relationship. She may never forget the comments.

Tension created during the match can continue to carry over for a long time. If one partner apologizes and the other partner doesn't buy the apology, anger may be harbored for weeks or months to come. Sweeping these issues under the rug for 20 years may eventually result in leaking toxicity.

Remember, forgiveness reigns. A spouse may do or say something that is mean and hurtful, but when an apology is made, choose to accept it for the good of yourself and the relationship. The key here is that the apology must be given and received in sincerity. A phony apology just never seems to be truly accepted.

Keys to Success
* *Know when to be competitive and when to back off.*

Chapter 10

Peter and Stacey
Round Two: Gluttons for Punishment?

D r. Clara stopped by the Daytons' house to catch up with Peter and Stacey. Peter answered the door.

"How are you?" she asked.

Peter replied, "Just completed about half the items on my Honey Do List and decided to take a lunch break." He had made himself his favorite sandwich, a turkey and Swiss with cranberry and cream cheese. He plopped down on the couch, turned on the TV and began channel surfing. "Let's watch some tennis," he said. He settled on a tennis network with hopes of catching a good match.

The match being shown was already late in the third set and quickly concluded. Up next was a special segment on strategy and psychology of playing mixed doubles. He was about to change the channel when a statement about playing and enjoying tennis with the opposite sex caught his ear.

"Wow," Dr. Clara said. "That's timely. How are you guys doing since your tennis match? I was squirming in my seat watching that."

"Well," Peter replied, "I think enough time has passed and the wounds have healed enough that Stacey and I can talk about it. Definitely need to before the second match at Ambrose. Even after we vented our frustrations with you after the match, things were still a little too raw to discuss whether we could put your suggestions into action."

"I think you should try," Dr. Clara remarked.

Later that day Peter got up the nerve to talk to Stacey about playing together again in their next match. They discussed what they had each learned from Dr. Clara, including the feelings and expectations of one another on the court. Stacey was skeptical about Peter not letting his competitiveness trump his ability to control his emotions but thought she would like the opportunity to play together again. She reluctantly agreed to give it another try in Round Two of the Ambrose Tournament.

The Round Two match was against Craig and Kim Zimmer, who were of a similar skill level. Peter and Stacey talked as they engaged in some pre-match stretching.

"I think I now understand that what I say to you during the match can be interpreted differently by you, and that if I feel the need to critique you, I should restrain myself and make only positive comments." said Peter.

"Critique me? That would be like a novice giving advice to a journeyman. How about not saying anything and just worry about your own game," Stacey replied, and then added, "I know what you meant—but probably not the best choice of words."

The match started off pretty well, with both Peter and Stacey keenly aware of each other's feelings. They had their share of unforced errors and tactical mistakes through the first few games. After five games the Zimmers were ahead 4-1, and Peter was sure his tongue had begun to swell from all the times he bit it rather than make negative comments to Stacey. In the sixth game, with Peter serving, the score 40-30, he served out wide to Craig who barely got his racquet on it and popped up an easy sitter to Stacey at the net.

Peter yelled, "Put it away, Stacey!"

She proceeded to hit the ball into the back fence on the fly. Peter just stood there with hands on hips staring at Stacey but saying nothing. The Zimmers won the next two points and the next game as the first set ended 6-1.

Between sets, while munching on an energy bar, Peter said,

"Wow, now that was ugly."

"If ugly means you are blaming me for your lackluster play, then yes, it was very ugly," said Stacey.

"Listen, Stacey, give me some credit. I thought I did a great job keeping my negative comments to myself," responded Peter.

"I saw the look of disdain on your face when I missed that easy put-away in the sixth game and caused you to lose your serve. I knew exactly what you were thinking, but you were too afraid to say anything!" replied Stacey.

"So, you're not going to cut me any slack for keeping my mouth shut when you choked on that easy sitter that could have gotten us back in the set? And it's not that I was afraid to say anything to you. It's that I was frustrated and knew I shouldn't say anything rather than saying something hurtful," said Peter.

"Let's finish discussing this after the match," replied Stacey.

As Peter was at the net awaiting Stacey's serve to start the second set, he thought to himself, "I have made conscious efforts not to make negative comments to Stacey during play, and she still isn't happy with me. I can't even look at her without her taking it the wrong way, I don't know what I'm supposed to do."

Having been fired up by their spirited discussion between sets, Stacey fired an ace to Kim, hit two winners and held serve easily. While switching ends of the court, Peter flashed back on some of Dr. Clara's advice and complimented Stacey on a strong service hold: "Way to take it to them. That's my girl."

"Thanks," said Stacey.

The set trudged along with both teams holding serve. With the score tied at 4-4 Peter gave Stacey a pep talk. "This is a huge game. If we win it, all the pressure will be on the Zimmers to prolong the match. Let's play smart, keep the ball in play, and let them make the mistakes."

"I'll do my best," Stacey replied.

The ninth game of the set began with a 23-shot rally. Peter, out of breath, tried to end the point with a winner from ten feet behind the baseline. His shot was easily picked off by Craig at the net and deposited for the point.

"Ahh—hello, Peter! Not a very high-percentage shot you hit given your position on the court. What happened to playing smart and letting them make the mistakes? You're not Rafa Nadal, you know," snapped Stacey.

Not wanting to admit he was out of breath, Peter responded, "I thought I could make the shot, so I went for it. I really hit it with a lot of pace, but Craig made an incredibly lucky defensive shot."

"Are you kidding me? I think you framed that ball. Craig couldn't wait for that beach ball to arrive, so he could deflate it. He barely had to move. It's okay to admit you made a mistake, but I think your ego won't let you." Stacey said scornfully.

"Let's both chill out before this escalates any further," replied Peter. The set ended with a 4-6 defeat.

As they walked to the parking lot Stacey asked Peter, "How do you think this match went? Do you think we made any headway as far as our compatibility on the court?"

"I know we were both trying to be conscious of each other's feelings, but once the competitive juices began to flow, it was hard to mask our emotions," answered Peter.

"Some of your reactions to my mistakes certainly weren't what I was hoping for, and I realize I still have work to do as well. The true test will be to see if we can control our emotions in our next match when there is more on the line," said Stacey.

"I thought I did a pretty good job of keeping my emotions in check today. Don't you?" Peter asked.

"I guess that depends what your definition of 'good' is. I am guardedly optimistic about playing with you in our match. Let's just see what happens," replied Stacey.

Chapter 11

Courtside Coaching: Let's Take a Breather
The Authors Offer a Deeper Look

"Seems like Dr. Clara thinks we're at a pivotal point where we either figure it out, or we don't," said Stacey.

"Yeah, if you try really hard, I think we can make this thing work," Peter chuckled under his breath.

"I can make it work. The question is can you make it work Peter?" said Stacey.

"Yeah, I know I need to take my eyes off of you and concentrate on my own game," replied Peter.

"When couples enter a competitive match, emotions can be difficult to control. Even couples who have played together may make comments that are hurtful. It's important to realize that heat-of-the-moment comments are just that, so try to refrain from making them, and try not to be so sensitive if you're on the receiving end," Dr. Clara had counseled.

"She's right. We both took shots at each other that weren't exactly complimentary," Stacey said.

"I get it. We need to be encouraging and not critical," Peter acknowledged.

Stacey continued, "As Dr. Clara said, we have got to realize that heat-of-the-moment comments are just that—we have all experienced situations when high tension or stressful moments cause us to say things we wouldn't ordinarily say. This can certainly happen on the tennis court. While hard to accept, we need to keep in mind that these comments are not a true representation of our feelings. Responding with another negative comment will only increase tension. Stay positive."

***

Recap

Know what you can expect from your partner; playing with your spouse doesn't necessarily mean you are playing with someone of your skill level. Know and understand the abilities and capabilities of your partner, and don't expect them to be exceeded. Be realistic with your expectations, and don't put undue pressure on your partner, especially when your opponent is clearly of a higher skill set.

Peter is still trying to control Stacey's game instead of paying attention to his own. He wants to win. This is his true character, and it is revealed as the pressure increases.

Mixed doubles can sure be difficult for some couples. As the match progressed, and the pressure of competition increased, Peter and Stacey were critical of one another, partially because competition knows no gender.

Stacey made scathing sarcastic remarks to defend herself, and because she is a competitive person, it wasn't surprising to see her stand her ground. This is the way she sets limits from someone else telling her what to do.

It's with waning confidence that Stacey begins to trust in Peter's new behavior. No doubt she knows it won't happen overnight. If his behavior becomes more consistent, she will trust him.

Keys to Success

- *Know what you can expect from your partner. Playing with your spouse doesn't necessarily mean you are playing with someone of your skill level.*

Chapter 12

Peter and Stacey
Round Three: Something Has Got to Give

The morning sun began to wash over the breakfast table where Peter and Stacey were chatting and enjoying their carbo-rich meal.

"The secret to winning today's match is these banana pancakes," joked Peter.

"Boy, I wish it was that simple," Stacey replied.

There was a current of nervous anticipation in the room—Round Three of the tournament had arrived.

"I think I'm going to take the D.S.S.S approach to today's match," said Peter.

"What does that stand for?" asked Stacey.

"It stands for Don't Sweat the Small Stuff!" exclaimed Peter. "I'm not going to let errors or mistakes by either of us change my positive outlook on the match. I want to have fun and enjoy our time together on the court. We take our physical health for granted but we are so lucky just to be able to run around on a tennis court. Let's keep things in perspective. Winning points or winning matches are really both small stuff."

Stacey stared at Peter for a few seconds, then said, "Who are you, and what have you done with Peter? That's a very healthy outlook," she continued, "and one I hope we both can adhere to."

"It will be a challenge," Peter acknowledged. "But if we both maintain the positive mindset Dr. Clara talked about, it will go a long way toward a better experience on the court."

The final match of the tournament had arrived and so had so

many uncomfortable memories of the couple's first experiences at the event. In the back of their minds both Peter and Stacey knew this could be a "make it or break it" experience for them. They both hoped for continuity and supportive play and couldn't stomach the thought of another court calamity.

On the drive to the tournament, Stacy wanted to talk about doubles strategy. "We need the advantage over our opponents, so try to remember what we learned in our clinics about—"

Peter interrupted Stacy before she had finished, "Listen, you're making my head spin. I don't want to think about anything besides being aggressive and trying to keep the ball in play."

"Okay, I'm sorry. You're right. That's small stuff," said Stacy.

"Just one more thing. Dr. Clara mentioned the idea of hitting a reset button. I think that would be helpful for me. Just a word or phrase that reminds me of what's important and why we are playing in the first place. We both can use it if we think the other is crossing the line," said Peter.

Stacey smiled again. "Okay, I agree. Any idea about what our reset should be?"

"Yes," said Peter. "'Scottsdale.' It's where we first met. When I think of those times, it brings me back to why I love being around you."

Stacey broke into an even bigger smile, "'Scottsdale' it is!"

They arrived for their 11 a.m. match at 10:30 and got on the court at 10:55. Typical of these events, they had very little time to warm up. Their opponents, Andy and Kate Daly, were already on the court stretching. Dr. Clara was in the stands enjoying the sun and looking forward to watching the match.

"This should be interesting," said Dr. Clara to herself. "We may see fireworks right here in the middle of the day."

Peter and Stacey won the coin toss and elected to serve. "Let's just have fun," Peter said to Stacey just before he tossed the ball in the air to begin the first set. Despite their best intentions, after just four games, with an anemic serving display by Peter and two missed overheads by Stacey, things weren't going the way they had envisioned. Peter was frustrated.

"Come on, Stacey, let's get these guys," Peter said.

"Are you blaming me?" said Stacey. She thought, "Here we go again." She couldn't help herself and said, "You are the one who can't seem to get a decent serve in."

"Me?" Peter replied. On the brink of a verbal eruption, he said, "Scottsdale" instead.

Much of the tension dissipated and they looked at each other with knowing smiles. They had hit the reset button and were in a better place. Stacey picked up quickly that Peter was on his best behavior and making serious attempts at civility. She decided to do her part in making this work. The match ended with a loss 2-6, 3-6 to the Daly's, but the chance of their playing together again did not.

"I like the 'don't sweat the small stuff' theory, Peter," said Stacey as they left the court.

"We both had our less than shining shots, poor decisions and executions, but I've finally come to realize we are always going to have them. We're not perfect. We're not machines. We are two people doing the best we can," said Peter.

Stacey added, "Plus, we shouldn't always interpret one another's comments as negative or hurtful. I think it's just the way we blow off steam or try to relieve pressure."

"Do we really need this strife in our relationship?" Peter said thoughtfully. "I've decided the answer is no! If I feel the need to trash talk or give someone grief on the court, I'll play with my buddies. They will give me crap, and I'll give it right back. When the match is over, we'll shake hands and go have a beer together, end of story. I'm not saying everything's always going to be perfect between you and me, but I do think we've come to an understanding on how to respect each other on the tennis court."

"I'm hoping today's experience wasn't just a fluke," Stacey

said. "But I feel, with our new awareness of expectations of each other, we can have many fun times together on the court, and that it will carry over to our off-court relationship as well!"

Chapter 13

Courtside Coaching: Don't Give Up
The Authors Offer a Deeper Look

Peter and Stacey talked to Dr. Clara. They met her at a table overlooking the courts.

"That came out better than I thought it would," Dr. Clara said.

"Yeah, it wasn't exactly perfect, but we got through it," Peter replied.

"We'll probably always banter back and forth. We may even lose our temper from time to time, but I like how it went today. What do you think Dr. Clara?" inquired Stacey.

"You two have shown that you can indeed play tennis successfully with each other. Of course, you'll have to continue to work and maintain your new-found revelations and attitudes, since we all tend to get lazy and fall back into old patterns of behavior," said Dr. Clara.

"Well, we may have a relapse from time to time, but we'll just have to work at trying to be the best we can," said Peter.

"You're right. This is a good start and it's up to us to work at it," Stacey piped in.

"Exactly," said Dr. Clara. "I know it sounds difficult to be 'on' all the time, monitoring yourself, and minding your manners, but successful relationships do take effort. If you two care enough to keep the threads of your tennis partnership from unraveling, you must continue implementing what you have learned as well as being open to learning."

***

Recap

Peter and Stacey found a device to keep things in check. They have a *reset button to keep the situation from getting* out of control. It's easy to tell when the tension level is reaching the point of someone saying or doing something they will regret. Be aware when you are nearing that point and activate the reset button. Agree ahead of time on what word or signal the reset button will be. It's a simple reminder that you are here to have fun. Use this button to defuse any impending negative outbursts or comments.

Stacey and Peter know things will not always be perfect between the two of them. They're both strung tight. However, Peter and Stacey understand that they can have a better experience playing together if they work on their mutual respect for each other in the heat of the battle.

Keys to Success

- *Have a reset button to keep the situation from getting out of control.*

Chapter 14

A Woman's Perspective: Cathy Carter

My husband and I have been playing the game of tennis for only 7 years and have been married for 28 years. We both come from a sports background and are familiar with coed sports such as baseball, softball, ping pong, and even game night with other couples. Yet nothing prepares you for the intensity of being on a tennis court with your spouse. I have always been enamored with how much of an athlete my husband is, and this ability is one of the things that attracted me to him. He can typically pick up any ball and be successful at that sport, so I knew in my heart that we would be a dynamic duo on the court. However, once the emotions begin to creep in, neither of us is our best self, and we change from a dynamic duo to struggling individuals.

As a couple, we know each other so well that with a word or some body language, we know where that person's disposition is. It can quickly tear the other person down. However, I think there is a secret there that men so often miss. Peter said something during his match that I would love to hear on the court, "Way to take it to them—that's my girl." In those few words, Peter has shown faith and respect for Stacey's level of play and claimed her as the woman of his dreams. Maybe a bit dramatic, but I don't believe overstated. That statement really resonated with me. Because of my respect for my spouse's athleticism, a compliment or acknowledgement from him could change my entire attitude and my level of play. In my opinion, the positive influence our spouses carry within them is not often used to their benefit. Don't we all want a gold star for our efforts in life? Who better to deliver that star than the person you love and respect the most?

In reading the story about Peter and Stacey, I enjoyed the suggestion of having a "reset word." That is a brilliant idea and one I'd like to immediately apply to us. In life, a memory or a song can always ground us with what our priorities should be and remind us of what's most important. Having a reset word would cause you to react and think about the bigger perspective on what's happening in the heat of the moment. That shared word may save other negative ones from being spoken. I'm pondering what our word could be as I write this.

If there is a long-term hope for Stacy and Peter to play together, I think that more would be gained by them not instructing each other during a match. Let a pro give the advice. If couples want to play together, once the match has begun, the court is the wrong place for instruction by one or the other. A lot can be gained by a pro watching a match, then having a clinic afterward that constructively helps their efforts at future matches. The men in these stories, however, assume they have superior tennis knowledge and try to instruct their partners. Having a pro do this could eliminate the tension of one of the partners trying to maintain the role of pro with the other. No one wants to be told what to do by someone who is not significantly better, male or female. It's a slippery slope in any tennis match, mixed or other, and shouldn't be tolerated. I know a lot of ladies who have more court time than their husbands, yet the male weekend warrior thinks his athletic ability and what he knows from watching the tennis channel trumps court time and experience. If you're planning on playing competitively together, leave the advice to the professionals and give only praise instead.

Is there an inner caveman in our man? I believe so. I perceive that men will try to protect and slay as needed to succeed—with a club, or, in this story, a tennis racquet. Maybe as women we need to understand that underlying instinct and develop a little thicker skin. They are not there to gather information from opponents and socialize with the other tennis players as we women do. They are there to do what men do, which is to hunt like a caveman. As it relates to tennis, men are the hunters, and the hunted is the opponent who they must kill/overcome to bring home the prize. It's this natural instinct that we women take as over-competitive. A bit of understanding that instinct could go a long way for women. Why can't we meld our differences, respecting the assets of both the hunter and the gatherer, in an attempt to achieve success?

As cavewomen, we are gatherers of information. On the courts, we women use that natural ability and assess our opponents. Understanding and overhearing a conversation, observing body language are all a sort of gathering of information we gals do to determine the opponent's strengths and weaknesses. Using our cavewoman attributes and an understanding of each other can foster mutual respect on the court.

When playing with someone who is not your spouse, there is an unspoken rule of being the best partner you can be while at the same time being on your best behavior. We tend to compliment them more, keep our feelings to ourselves, and maybe focus a little bit more. We even try a little harder so as not to be embarrassed by our level of play; we want to hold up our half of the court and not let our partner down. Yet do we do that when playing with our spouse? Could that make a difference? Maybe Peter or any of us would benefit by applying these mindsets when playing with our spouse. Could that potentially bring a new respect and appreciation for how lucky we are to play with them?

I believe my spouse and I are equally competitive. Yet our personality styles and what motivates us on the court can be entirely different. In a match, I want to win just as much as he does. As I said, I see my spouse as one of the most athletic men I know, but our differences in what motivates us and pushes our hot buttons makes it not worth the repercussions and aftermath at home. Yet I have to ask, could the shoe be on the other foot? In writing this, I must confess, have I asked what motivates him? Do I do things that tear him down on the court? What can I do to help the success of our results on the court, win or lose? Am I asking the same questions myself that I expect him to consider for me? We all have mixed troubles from time to time, but I'm hoping for long-term successful doubles with my husband.

Chapter 15

Brayden & Katie
Round One: Ignite the Fireworks

In the last chapter, Cathy poses a good question: "Do I do things that tear him down on the court?" You'll achieve better results, win or lose, when you build your partner up. Players need reassurance when they're playing well, not just when they're having a rough time. A little positive assurance that things will be all right will go a long way.

We have another couple of characters we'd like you to meet, Brayden and Katie Brees. Brayden is a competitive person to the point where it affects his emotions. Katie is passive and struggles with setting limits. The combination is a recipe for disaster. We'd like to show you how their experience can change if Brayden turns down the heat, and Katie draws a line in the sand.

***

Brayden Brees fell head over heels for Katie the moment he saw her. They met when she stopped by his tradeshow booth at an industry function and introduced herself. After a few minutes of conversation, Brayden got up the nerve to ask Katie out for lunch, and she accepted.

They rendezvoused at the Daily Grill and had a wonderful time as lunch slipped into the cocktail hour. They learned a lot about each other. He enjoyed sports and strove to succeed at whatever he did. Katie enjoyed gardening, cooking, staying fit and being in the company of family and good friends. While he was sipping Maker's Mark and she a cosmopolitan, a mutual interest in tennis came up. They agreed to meet the following Wednesday at the local high school tennis courts. One year later he proposed, and she accepted.

They purchased their first home in the San Francisco East Bay Area. One evening, sitting by the fire, they were reminiscing fondly about the times they had enjoyed playing tennis together and rallying back and forth. They began to talk about traveling and playing in a tournament one day. Eventually, they decided to participate in the Ambrose Tournament. The events leading up to their first clash, we mean match, went like this:

"What level do you think we should play?" Katie asked.

"We've played off and on and had a couple of group lessons together. I recall our instructor suggesting that you're a 3.5 bordering 4.0 and I'm a 4.0. We should start at the Mixed 7.5 Level and see how we do," Brayden suggested.

"All right—agreed! I'm signing us up online now. Let's get out and practice—if we're going to compete in this tournament we should go for the win!" replied Stacey.

"Okay. But I hope we can meet some nice people as well. You know my folks have developed quite a few friendships as a result of playing tennis. Does playing at 1:00 p.m. today work for you?" asked Brayden.

"Yes, that works for me. I can't wait to get out there and hit the ball back and forth—the tournament is next weekend."

The tournament weekend finally arrived, and Brayden and Katie were eager to get started.

"Hello, we're here to check in. I'm Brayden Brees and this is my wife, Katie."

"Good afternoon and here you go, Mr. and Mrs. Brees. This is your player packet with instructions and match schedules. You'll be playing in a round robin format. Your first match is at 1:30 p.m. on court three. We're running just slightly behind schedule. You can start warming up at 1:20 p.m. if the court is available. Good luck!" said the woman at the front desk.

"Thank you. We really enjoyed Dr. Clara's presentation last night. She's here to observe our match. We're excited and look forward to the fun," replied Katie.

"Yeah—the competition too," Brayden chimed in. "Come on, Katie—let's go see if we can warm-up someplace. It's an advantage being loose, warm, and ready to go."

"Well, why don't you go and hit against the backboard? I don't need much warm-up, and I'd like to look around. I'll meet you on court 3 at 1:20 p.m.," Katie said.

"All right—see you then," Brayden confirmed

Brayden walked over to the backboard area and started stretching. He felt agitated that Katie wasn't interested in a thorough warm-up. "Now it's probably going to take her at least three games to get going," he thought to himself. "That could be the difference in the match. I already know I'm going to have to carry her and try to get to every ball. I think I'll give her a few things to think about before the match gets under way."

As Brayden stretched, Dr. Clara walked by. "Hi, Brayden," Dr. Clara said. "I'm looking forward to watching your match."

"Hello, Dr. Clara," Brayden replied. "We hope to give you a good show!"

Katie arrived for their match full of energy and ready to go, looking great in her new tennis outfit. She was enjoying being part of this event, meeting other people, and chatting with tennis vendors.

"Come on, Katie, let's get onto the court and start warming up," Brayden said.

"Sounds good. Let's go play our best," she enthusiastically replied.

"You bet! But let's concentrate on winning just one point at a time. I want you to focus on your groundstroke follow through. You probably should lay off the overheads—that's a low-odds shot for you. And try to get your first serve up the middle. Sound good?" Brayden said.

Katie appeared a little taken aback by Brayden's unsolicited advice, but it didn't seem to bother her. "Sounds good," she half-heartedly replied.

Their opponents walked onto the court. They all shook hands, warmed up, spun the racquet for side or serve, and the match got under way.

"We look pretty good. Let's pound the lady. I think it will give us a better chance. Let's try to run 'em. I know we're in better shape. Come on, Katie. Our mantra will be 'skill and will, let's go do it,'" said Brayden.

"I'm nervous enough playing in this game," Katie thought. "Now Brayden's putting more pressure on me, I know he wants to win, but doesn't he think I want to win too?" They had elected to serve first, so she collected her thoughts.

Katie quickly double-faulted the first two points away, game score love-30. Brayden was frustrated and mumbled to himself, "Can't she just dink it over the net? What's so hard about that? That's what happens when you don't warm up. I know I'm the stronger player, and I can see I'm going to have to take charge. We still can win this game." He shouted at Katie, "Come on, you can do it. Work on that toss!"

Katie's next serve went in. The opponent hit a cross-court return back to her. She lobbed back, but too deep, and now the game score was love-40. They went on to lose the next point and the first game. After they moved to change sides, Brayden had more advice for Katie.

"Well, we've got the first game behind us. Let's win the next one. You might not want to lob as much. Several of them went long. If you do, put more topspin on the ball to bring it down. Better yet, just hit out." Brayden said.

They had a few sips of water and went back onto the court. The second game didn't go much better than the first. They were down love-2 and it was now Brayden's turn to serve.

He hit a good first serve, and the opponent returned it to

Katie. She attempted a volley but hit into the net. She looked back at Brayden and could see by his body language that he was frustrated with her. "I know I can do better," she thought to herself. Brayden continued to serve, and they won the next two points, game score 30-15.

"Come on—one point at a time," he said to her.

"What does he mean by that? He's getting on my nerves."

Brayden continued to serve well, but it just wasn't enough. They lost the game and went on to lose the next one, too. They were down love–4, and it was Katie's serve.

Before her serve Brayden thought to himself, "I need to get to every ball, It's the only way."

Katie got her serves in, and Brayden was able to get into good court position. They won the first two points. Katie was serving at 30-0, but when she double-faulted Brayden walked over to her and told her to keep her head up and watch the ball. The game continued as she got her serves in. Brayden made a couple of great shots, and they won the game—match score 1-4.

During the changeover, Katie took a drink of water and Brayden sipped on a sports drink; he suggested that she have some of it—that way she would have more energy on the court. She said water is what she liked, but she was thinking, "Am I really that sluggish out there?"

Game 6 was under way. They dropped the first point on an unforced error by Katie, and Brayden looked over at her and said, "Hey, don't hit that shot—you haven't made it all day." Katie was embarrassed, knowing that the opposing team had heard the comment. Brayden was convinced that he really needed to take over the match. "Man, in school I used to kick butt on the court. Now we're getting spanked. I gotta do something about this. The other team is a little older than we are, and I'm much stronger than Katie. I need to kick it up a notch," he thought.

Brayden was trying to get to every ball and hit bigger and

better shots, but the harder he tried, the more mistakes he made. He moved to hit an easy cross-court shot but overpowered it, and it went out. Katie looked at him and yelled, "You're playing way out of control—tone it down a little." That comment infuriated Brayden. He tried even harder but to no avail as they lost the first set 1-6.

"Well, that didn't go very well," Brayden said at the change-over. "What do you think we should do differently in the next set?"

"For starters you can stop telling me what to do. I can hear those heavy sighs coming from you when I make a mistake. Don't you think I feel bad and want to make my shots?" said Katie.

"I'm just trying to give you a few tips to help turn this around," replied Brayden.

"Save your tips. I don't want them. Let's get back onto the court." Katie was not happy.

"Okay, let's go do it, skill and will. Since I'm the stronger server I'll serve first," Brayden said.

"Whatever. If that's what you want, be my guest," replied Katie.

They played better the first five games of the second set, and at the changeover, the match score was 2-3. "Come on, good playing. This is a big game—we can tie it up 3-3 or we can go down 2-4. Let's follow the ball, take the net, and communicate. Come on!" said Brayden.

The sixth game got under way, and Katie was aced. Brayden looked over at her. "Just watch the ball and stick your racquet out. Try it," he said.

He received the second serve and made a nice return. The opponent hit to Katie. She hit a weak shot short and up front. The opposing woman nailed it for a cross-court winner. Brayden shrugged his shoulders and let out a sigh of disgust. "Follow-through high!" he shouted and slammed his racquet into the net. "Jeez, this is a train wreck."

Katie placed her hands on her hips and looking like a drill sergeant yelled, "Don't tell me what to do! Say nothing to me the rest of this match! Nothing!"

They went on to lose the game, set, and match. They slung their tennis bags over their shoulders and walked off the court, silent and frustrated.

Chapter 16

Courtside Coaching: Extinguish the Flame
The Authors Offer a Deeper Look

D r. Clara greeted them at a picnic table near the south lawn. "You two look like you're ready to explode. What happened out there?" Dr. Clara asked.

"I can't believe how Brayden behaved. His mannerisms and comments made me feel terrible," Katie responded.

"Well I'm in this thing to win. It's frustrating when things don't go our way," snapped Brayden.

"Our way, don't you mean your way," retorted Katie?

"Did you guys talk about the match before you walked onto the court?" Dr. Clara asked.

"What do you mean talk about the match? What's there to talk about?" replied Brandon.

"Well for starters, what you expect from your experience playing in the match. It's a psychological advantage for your team knowing what your partner may be thinking before you walk onto the court," replied Dr. Clara.

"How so?" inquired Katie.

"It puts you in a better position to anticipate and prepare for what may occur during your match. Having a mutual understanding of what each person wants from a match is an important component of playing together," said Dr. Clara.

"Yeah, Brayden, it's like picking a restaurant for dinner. We usually ask each other what we feel like having, and then choose the restaurant," Katie said.

"Exactly," replied Dr. Clara. "Brayden you looked pretty intense out there. Can you tell us why?"

"Hell yes, I thought I needed to carry the match. I'm the stronger player," said Brayden.

"Stronger headed," chimed in Katie.

"Call it what you like, I was focused on winning," said Brayden.

"Let's talk about that for a minute. My observation is that before the match started you knew you were the stronger player, and felt you had to carry the match. This put pressure on yourself before the match had even started. When the match was not going your way, your mindset wavered, which led to negative comments and unsolicited advice. Katie did not appreciate it," said Dr. Clara.

"You got that right," replied Katie in a testy voice.

"Ok, I think I get it. I need to think about my own game," said Brayden.

"Correct," confirmed Dr. Clara. "Katie, why did you wait until tempers flared to tell Brayden you were becoming angry with his comments?"

"Well, it just caught up with me I guess," Katie said. "I should have said something earlier. I never have a problem telling him how I feel at home."

"Katie, you must set a boundary with Brayden at the first sign of insult and tell him to stop. It takes practice for all of us to learn to set limits early. We tend to let small things slide to avoid conflict but oftentimes then they become a larger issue. Limits break down under pressure, and defense systems go up. It's easy to blow out a match, but harder to blow out a forest fire," said Dr. Clara.

***

Recap

Brayden and Katie go into the game with their own mental agendas. Brayden wants to go for the win and is focused on winning at all costs, including the expense of hurting others. We heard him say, "Let's pound the woman." Katie wants to socialize and meet people. They could not be further apart on their expectations for the match.

It's a mental benefit for your team knowing what each person may be thinking before a match starts. Having a mutual understanding of what each person wants from a match is an important component of playing together. When we know how we each feel about something, then we know how to support the desired outcome. When Katie and Brayden focus on their common goals, they become a united front and have a better opportunity to accomplish their goals. If there is no focus and direction, there is chaos, impulsiveness, tension, and more than likely, poor results.

Before the match, Brayden had already decided Katie was the weaker player and that he would need to carry her. This put a lot of pressure on him before the match had even started. Pressuring Katie to control her performance has the opposite of the intended effect. It actually increases her nervousness, negatively affecting her performance. It would be much more supportive for Brayden to be thinking of his own game, being aware of what he can do to play better, and being accepting of his partner's skill level. He would be more effective offering support through positive comments. Maintaining an open mindset is an opportunity to learn to play better individually and as a team. Why does Brayden have to pressure Katie if he is focused on his own game? He may be trying to blame her or others (not himself) because of the impending undesired outcome.

Katie is able to ignore Brayden's first comment, but anger is festering. Brayden continues offering unsolicited advice, which angers her and elevates her stress level. Katie must set limits with Brayden. It may take some getting used to for all of us to learn to set boundaries before tempers escalate. We tend to let minor things slide to avoid conflict but oftentimes then they escalate into a larger issue. Limits break down under pressure, and defense systems go up. Each person must communicate and set limits on his or her partner's behavior early on, before it builds up to an explosion, and someone walks off the court. Late in the match, Katie does set a boundary, telling Brayden to save his tips and not tell her what to do. Mentally and emotionally, she is distraught and not up for another self-esteem hit from Brayden.

Finally, because of to the pressure he has placed on himself Brayden feels he must "take charge" and tell Katie what to do.

However, people do not want to be controlled. In fact, most of us detest it. The resulting fallout is that Katie becomes filled with self-doubt and begins second-guessing herself. She has hurt feelings and is embarrassed. The match has evolved into a humiliating experience for her, and she resents Brayden and his behavior.

Keys to Success
- *Develop mutual expectations for your match.*
- *It's such an uncomfortable feeling when spouses are mad at each other. It doesn't matter if you're the one who's upset, or the one who's on the receiving side. It's best to provide encouragement.*
- *Set boundaries early with your partner. This reduces the chance of the small things we let go developing into all-out war.*
- *Be aware of your own game and how you play.*
- *Be accepting of your partner's game—and that it might be as good as it gets.*
- *It's best to only give advice when requested by your partner.*

Chapter 17

Brayden and Katie
Round Two: Try it Again—Will Practice Make Perfect?

Couples must recognize that it takes real commitment to change behavior. When patterns of behavior have been ingrained in our psyche, the response they produce during a mixed doubles match may be counterintuitive. We may say or respond in a manner that is not supportive. The funny thing is often we know our actions will produce a negative response, yet we do it anyway. Why? The good news is that when we become aware of this behavior, we can begin to hone ourselves into supportive partners. Let's pick up our story where we left off: Can Brayden temper his competitive nature? Will Katie set limits and communicate if they are crossed?

***

Katie broke the uncomfortable silence that had paralyzed them since they walked off the court.

"That's the point," she murmured in a shaken voice.

"What's the point? What do you mean?" Brayden asked.

"The point is that everything Dr. Clara shared with us is right-on. We walked into this tennis match together. We walked off the court together, and we're here together. Let's get this figured out and get back out there and play together," Katie said.

"I would love to," Brayden acknowledged in a conciliatory tone. "I want this to be fun for us. I will do my best not to let the match get the best of me—ultimately us."

"Are you sure? It's as if you were a different person out there.

Certainly not the man I thought I married," Katie said.

"Yes, I'm sure. I want this to be fun, and I want to win too. I'm sorry I made you feel so uncomfortable. I love playing with you. I'll try my best to put winning a little further down our playing agenda. I like meeting new people and making friends too! I understand our goal is to play our best, have fun, win, and meet people—right?" Brayden asked.

"Not quite, sweetheart," Katie said. "We need to put people ahead of winning—okay?"

His attentiveness to Katie drifted away for a moment. He was rapidly replaying in his mind the conversation they had had with Dr. Clara: "Don't slam your spouse like you would the tennis ball." These words resonated loud and clear with him. He knew the right thing to do, and it was not to tell Katie what to do! He said to himself, "I will try to refrain from giving her any advice unless she asks me for it—but I doubt she will. I know I need to be positive and not say anything judgmental. Otherwise, it will put her into a tailspin."

"Hello? Hello, Brayden. Come in—did you hear me?" said Katie.

"Yes, I did. I was just thinking about our discussion, and I will do my best not to be your 'coach on the court.' I understand it makes you nervous and puts you under added pressure," said Brayden.

"Thank you. I think you get it. I'm not as strong a player as you are, and I need to stay confident," said Katie.

Brayden paused for a moment as a thought flashed through his mind. "She's right about everything, but I know, when we're on the court, I'm still going to have to carry her. I'm sure I can do this and still be supportive."

"All right. I'm looking forward to our match," said Brayden.

They arrived at their next match. "I'm ready to go—skill and will, let's go do it!" Brayden shouted. At the same time, in the back of his mind he was thinking, "We'll have fun, and there's nothing more fun than winning!"

"Another beautiful day for tennis," Katie said in her enthusiastic voice.

"Absolutely. This weather will allow our muscles to warm up faster and stay loose. I think Dr. Clara is going to see a different 'Team Brees' today," said Brayden.

After checking in, they made their way to court four. Brayden opened the gate for Katie and gave her a quick kiss. They placed their tennis bags on a wooden bench, grabbed their racquets, and walked onto the court. They introduced themselves to their opponents at the net, took positions for warm-ups, and then spun the racquet for side or serve.

The match got under way. Katie and Brayden had agreed earlier that Brayden would serve. They exchanged fist bumps and Katie trotted to her position at the net. She looked back at Brayden and whispered, "Good luck. Let's get it done."

He served well, and Katie bounced around at the net missing some and making some. They won the first game, and then met at the wooden bench during the exchange of sides.

"Nice serving sweetheart. That ace was a beauty," said Katie.

"Thanks! You played well too. You might want to think about faking a poach or two when you're at the net. It helps distract the person returning the serve," said Brayden.

Brayden could tell by the look in her eyes that his comment caught her a little off guard, but she chimed back, "You got it." She thought to herself, "Man! We just won the first game, and he's already telling me what to do."

The set score quickly advanced to 3-3. The all-important seventh game was under way, and Katie was at the service line. Brayden walked over to her and said confidentially, "These guys on the other side of the net don't have anything we don't have. I'm going to try harder to put balls away at the net and score points for us."

"Okay—you do that," Katie said.

Katie's thought process began to slip away from focusing on doing her best to not losing. She tossed the ball in the air and hit her first serve into the net. The second serve produced the same result—double fault. Brayden trotted over and extended his fist. Katie acknowledged, and they did the bump.

"Shake it off, no problem, one point at a time, we can do it," Brayden said.

Katie was starting to feel a little anxious as she hit her first serve to the ad court. It was a good serve, and Brayden was able to get his racquet on the opponent's return for a put-away. "Nice volley!" she shouted. Katie continued to serve defensively. She felt wobbly and tried to take deep breaths to control her nerves. However, it was all to no avail, and they wound up losing the game, set score 3-4.

Brayden walked over to the bench, grabbed a towel, and buried his face in it, all the time trying to think how he could take over the match. "How could she have lost her serve?" he thought. "All she had to do was get it in, and then I would work my butt off for the put-away."

He felt a nudge from Katie. "Sorry I served so poorly," she said. "I was really tight and nervous. I know you want to win. You think the guys on the other side of the net stink and you must think I do too."

Brayden's heart plunged directly to the middle of his stomach. He thought, "I can't bear the thought that I'm putting so much pressure on her. She must feel terrible. I really wanted a win for both of us, but particularly Katie. I wanted her to experience the thrill of winning a competitive match. What I was communicating was being perceived as the opposite." He slid the towel down his face, draped it behind his neck, and reached over and grabbed Katie's hand.

"Honey, I don't think you stink. I like being out here with you. I'm working hard trying to control myself. I apologize if I've hurt your feelings. Let's spend the rest of this match doing our best and have fun doing it. We lose a few points here and there, so what?" Brayden said.

"Okay, sweetheart. I like being out here with you, too. Let's chat it up out there and play our best. By the way, the guy has a weak backhand." Katie said.

"That's what I'm talking about, babe. Let's go do it!" Brayden exclaimed.

They walked onto the court with a new sense of purpose. They played well and fought off several ad points. Brayden felt calm, and Katie felt liberated. It showed as they went on to win the set 6-4, match score 1-1 and going to the tie-breaker.

During the exchange Katie went to fill her cup at the water cooler. The chilled water was refreshing. The guy from the other team was there as well. His weary eyes focused on Katie's and he said, "You guys sure played well those last three games. You got to my backhand and scored points. My wife kept trying to correct my stroke, but the more she criticizes me, the harder I try, and, the harder I try, the worse I perform. Good luck out there in the tie-breaker."

Katie shook her head in empathy. "Wow, I know what's it's like to be in that guy's tennis shoes. I wish him luck." She walked over to join Brayden as the court monitor was instructing them to resume play.

The first point in the tie-breaker went quickly. The score was 1-0, with Brayden and Katie ahead, and the tie-breaker on serve. Their opponents were due to serve next. Katie and Brayden walked over to the wooden bench.

"You're playing great, Katie. Let's keep the pressure on," Brayden said.

"Okay—you're doing well, too. Let's keep playing our game," Katie said.

They walked briskly onto the court and took their positions, Brayden on the ad side and Katie playing the deuce side. She crouched down in position to receive the serve. It came in hot, and she was aced. The score advanced to 2-2. Brayden began to feel the tension build. He figured he needed to smack a winner to gain the momentum. The woman serving looked into the service box, picked her spot, and then let it go. She hit a spinning serve that broke into his body. He tried to hit a big backhand, but the ball was met by the net. The error set him off, and he slammed his racquet onto the court in disgust. His violent reaction made Katie cringe, but she hung in there as the tie-breaker score went to 2-3.

"Come on, let's do it here," he shouted to Katie. "We can do it!"

Katie served, and the opponent's return of serve came in high and two feet to the left of the service line, just perfect for Brayden's forehand. He struck the ball with the sweet spot of his racquet and hit a strong return. The opponent got his racquet on it but could only produce a weak short lob return. Katie got into position for the easy overhead.

"This is it," Brayden thought. "We'll get another point." Katie did everything right in the execution of her shot except that she took her eye off the ball at impact. She blew the shot and dumped the ball into the net. It was more than Brayden could tolerate. He gave her a look of disgust, and the positive chatter they had come to enjoy was now on "mute."

He struggled with the conversation they had had before the match but convinced himself that now he had to insert himself into a position on the court to hit as many shots as he could while limiting Katie to the number of balls that might be hit to her. On his serve, he instructed Katie to stand in the corner while he was serving and that he would follow the ball in. He told her that she should cover any balls that came her away. She reluctantly agreed, immediately feeling inferior and wondering how he could be so smug. However, the strategy worked, and they won the point.

Once again, they met at the wooden bench. Brayden was

excited about the score and said in a pumped-up voice, "Great playing, Katie. You made some great shots, especially the lob to the ad side. Way to go. We won't have a chance to talk until the next four points are played. How you feeling? What do you think?"

"Well, this isn't like trying to win Wimbledon for me," Katie said. "You're too amped up. It makes me feel uncomfortable. I like winning points too, but what's with the slamming the racquet thing and trying to take over like General Patton? Let's just get out there and stay focused on playing our best."

"Okay, okay, I apologize. I'll try to stay centered around being positive and hope for the best," said Brayden.

"Well, you better! Let's go. It's time to start," Katie said.

The tie-breaker resumed. Both sides of the net played well. The tie-breaker score was now 7-6 with team Brees up by one point.

"Nice playing. Come on—reach deep and give me some! Let's keep pounding the guy's backhand and directing as many balls to him as we can. She's not the best volleyer, so we may want to bust one or two big ones at her. And by the way: You're awesome," Brayden said.

"Great—I'm with you. You're playing terrific tennis," said Katie.

Katie gazed over at her opponents and could see the guy getting an earful from his partner. She felt sorry for him but shook it off as Brayden shouted, "Skill and will, come on. Let's go do it."

It was his serve again, and again he instructed Katie on how he wanted her to play. He hit a good kick serve, and the opponent returned a weak shot back to Katie. She hit a lob back but left it a little low. The net person got hold of it and put it away for a winner—tie-breaker tied, 7-7.

Brayden looked over at Katie and told her to just hit out and forget about the lob. However, his instructions landed on deaf ears. Katie was in no mood to be told what to do. His unsought advice infuriated her so much that she shut down all communication between the two of them.

Brayden took over, running around like a madman on the court trying to make big plays. It was effective, and the tie-breaker score was now 8-7 in their favor.

"This is it," Brayden said. "Let's stay focused. Play like we're down 7-8. Just hit out—the serve is coming to you."

"'Stay focused'? Does he think I can't see?" Katie thought. "I don't like it when he tells me to hit out. Isn't it better to 'hit in' and keep the ball in play? What a maniac—the way he's running all over the place."

They took their positions. The guy was serving to Katie, and he was visibly nervous. His eyes, meeting Katie's, reflected a mutual level of discomfort. He tossed the ball and hit his serve wide and into the alley—fault. His wife ran over to him with her body language projecting strong disapproval. She angrily trotted back to the net, muttering, "Come on." His concentration was shaken. He focused on his serve for a moment and then threw up a weak toss and struck the ball. It sailed over the net and three feet out—double fault, match over. Katie and Brayden won the tie-breaker 9-7 and the match 2-1.

Instead of jubilation, the uncomfortable tension that had gripped them before the match had crept back in. They awkwardly exchanged fist bumps and a weak embrace and then met their opponents at the net to shake hands.

"What's the matter, Katie? Why the long face? We just won the match!" Brayden said.

"You still don't get it, do you? I know you're a stronger player, but I resent the fact that you stuck me in the corner when you were serving. It makes me feel like a little kid in timeout. I can actually play well, you know? Then, to make matters worse, you run all over the court like a Tasmanian devil—and what's with the racquet-throwing? That's so immature. You're good but not that good! If this is what it takes to win, then I'm damn sure I don't like it," Katie said.

Brayden felt terrible. He'd known his behavior would upset Katie, but he just couldn't help it—he did it anyway. "I'm an idiot ," he thought. He didn't know how to process his frustration, and the end result hurt Katie.

Chapter 18

Courtside Coaching: Healing Wounds
The Authors Offer a Deeper Look

"Katie you seemed upset after the win. What happened on the court?" Dr. Clara asked at their debrief session.

"I was a jerk out there," Brayden quickly interjected.

"That's an understatement. You were a tyrant. It's not your business to be telling me what to do," Katie said.

"Brayden you made a pact early on, but then you had trouble honoring it. Your ego still got the best of you. It appeared you were self-centered—focusing on yourself and not on the team. Is that a fair observation?" inquired Dr. Clara.

There was a moment of silence as Brayden struggled with the question, then Katie piped in, "Would you like me to answer that question for you?"

"No, I'm sorry, I guess my ego did get in the way," Brayden said.

"You guess, or you know?" Katie asked.

"Well I suppose I know, but I just didn't know what to do with my feelings," Brayden responded.

"It takes time and practice to adapt to new behavior. You have to reach deep down inside and change your belief system and integrity level. This can be difficult, but you can do it," Dr. Clara responded. "Katie, please tell Brayden how his actions affect you."

"You hurt my feelings, Brayden. I know you're the better player but I'm trying my best. That's all I can do," said Katie.

"I'm sorry, I really didn't want that to happen," replied

Brayden somberly.

"Brayden, you were not honoring your commitment to Katie. Your actions, although well-intended, hurt Katie's feelings. Subsequently you made another vow to Katie to let go of winning and focus on having fun and playing your team's best, but you broke that one too. Please understand that Katie may have trouble believing you. She's going to wonder next time: Is this just another empty promise?" said Dr. Clara. "Katie, how did his action affect you? Look at Brayden and tell him."

"Sometimes when you would say positive or encouraging things it made me feel great, like wow, you really like playing with me. However, then you'd roll your eyes or throw your racquet and it would make me feel inferior, like I blew it and you just didn't want to play with me," said Katie.

"Brayden, do you see how your actions were sending mixed signals to Katie?" Dr. Clara asked.

"Yes, I tried to say positive things, but at the same time I was sending mixed signals by giving her looks of disgust. Slamming my racquet into the court didn't help either," replied Brayden.

"Yeah, and what's with the advice out there? I didn't ask for it, and every time you gave it to me it made me angrier," said Katie.

"I was just trying to help us win more points," replied Brayden.

"Well, ticking me off is not a good way to do that," said Katie.

"Katie, my advice for you is to set limits with Brayden before your next match. Develop an expectation of what you will accept and what you won't tolerate. Brayden, rein in your ego a little and be aware of your behavior both verbally and physically. Practice these things. Learn to get better at them and you guys will have a much better time playing together," said Dr. Clara.

***

Recap

Brayden made several commitments, but he had trouble honoring them. His ego still got the best of him.

New behaviors may take time to develop. Sometimes you really have to work at it. You have to reach deep down inside and change your belief system and integrity level. First, you have to value your beliefs from the inside, then your actions will reflect what you honestly believe. Did he really buy into the new approach?

Brayden was still offering Katie unsolicited advice. His comments redirect Katie from concentrating on doing her best to concentrating on not losing—big difference. The pressure builds, and Brayden's actions produce the opposite result as she makes more errors. Every time she makes an error, it redirects her mentally to focus on not making another error. It's a no-win cycle that Katie can't break out of.

Brayden was not honoring his promise to Katie. His actions, although well-intended, hurt Katie's feelings. He made another vow to Katie to let go of winning and focus on having fun and playing their best. But he struggled with this one too. Katie may now have trouble believing him: Does he really mean it, or is he just saying it? Brayden's actions must now speak louder than words. It's his moment of truth. Katie can be supportive by understanding his lack of control on the tennis court but must still draw personal limits. She may be less judgmental knowing Brayden is at least trying to control himself.

Brayden's actions were sending mixed signals to Katie. He tried to say positive things but at the same time was giving her looks of disgust and slamming his racquet into the court. He needed to stop, think, and relax. Some people need a filter between their thoughts and their mouth. Allowing a moment of time to pass is sometimes the only way to accomplish self-control.

Physical reactions can be even stronger than verbal communication. Actions can breed resentment in the person receiving them, and resentment can soon turn into lingering suspicion and lack of trust. Sometimes physical responses may even frighten a partner. Brayden needs to be congruent in his communication. His facial expressions and body language must jibe with his words to transfer positive vibes to Katie.

Brayden thought he was too good to fail and began to give Katie unsolicited directions. His well-intended action becomes a recipe for disaster. Katie felt hurt. Finally, as a result of the tension, she lashes out and tells Brayden, "You're good, but you're not that good." Katie allowed her resentment to fester into a "time bomb". That, of course, hurts his feelings. It was a personal hit. Now his mind drifts from the match as he's processing the comment and trying to recover from the hit. A better approach for Katie would be to critique his actions not the person. Better yet, Katie needs to set clear limits with Brayden before the match has even started. A prerequisite is for Katie to clarify what behavior is acceptable, and more importantly, what behavior is not tolerable. She needs to make it clear to Brayden how his actions make her feel. Brayden needs to play within the lines on the court while not crossing the lines that upset Katie.

Keys to Success

- *It takes time and practice to adapt to new behavior. First, you have to value your beliefs from the inside, then your actions will reflect what you honestly believe. It takes real commitment.*
- *Be aware of your verbal and non-verbal communications.*
- *Try to ascertain what makes your partner tick. This way, it will be easier to understand his or her actions.*
- *Giving unsolicited advice may produce undesirable results.*
- *Set clear limits as to what behavior will not be tolerated.*

Chapter 19

Round Three: Will Brayden & Katie
Live to Play Another Day?

People like to be around positive people. Positive energy can make people feel better about themselves. It isn't any different on the tennis court. Being positive and supportive are paramount in mixed doubles. These qualities work wonders under all situations, winning or losing, stressed or unstressed, and happy or disgusted with your partner. So, stay positive—think, "Don't worry, be happy." Let's see if Brayden and Katie manage to walk off the court looking forward to the next time they play together.

***

"Brayden, it's amazing how Dr. Clara put everything into perspective. I get what she's saying. This really is a process—behavior doesn't change overnight," Katie said.

"I see how she wants us to play together and enjoy this game," Brayden responded. "I choose to get out there now and have fun with you!"

"I know we've played in one match where we lost the match, and we both lost emotionally. We've played another match where we won the match but lost emotionally. Let's see if we can put it all together and win emotionally, and perhaps the match as well. I believe it's possible. Skill and will, let's go do it!" said Katie.

"I've never felt more prepared to play with Katie," Brayden thought. "We're aligned mentally and have a mutual game plan.

I'm aware of what I say verbally and non-verbally and how it affects Katie. I have an inner-character awareness to help me channel my actions and responses in a positive way. I need to respond to the situation in ways that support my partner. I think I have a more realistic expectation of our play and—"

His thoughts were interrupted by the "swoosh" sound as he opened a new can of balls. He glanced down at one of the brand-new balls, a Pro Penn Number 4. "Huh," he thought. "My mindset used to be that the '4' stood for 'for winning.' Now I look at it as 'for fun.' I'm going to do my best 'for winning but not at the expense of fun with Katie."

"Let's go, Brayden! We won the racquet spin, so it's your serve. You're the man. Nothing but aces," Katie called to Brayden.

"I love it when she says things like that that," Brayden thought. "It makes me want to do better than my best."

They played sound tennis. They moved well on the court, stayed competitive in each point, and didn't make a lot of errors. They were equally matched with their opponents. The set score advanced to 4-4, and it was Brayden's turn to serve. He signaled Katie to meet him at the baseline.

"You're playing great, Katie—keep it up. This is a tight one. I've been pounding their backhands, and now I'm going to mix it up a little. I plan to take each one wide on the first serve. Hopefully we can catch them off guard and get them to dump the return into the net, or hit a dink shot that floats up a sitter," said Brayden.

"Got it," she said, and gave him a little pat on the tush before trotting back to the net.

His first serve was effective, and the ball didn't come back over the net. He set up for his next serve and delivered a great shot. The opponent got his racquet on it and popped it back to Katie. She moved forward and struck the ball, but harder than she needed to, and it sailed out of play. Brayden felt the pressure in his arm mount as he squeezed his racquet handle in anger. But he quickly reflected on what he'd learned. "Honest mistake—can't say I've never done that," he thought. "It's only one point. Let's move on to the next one." He gestured for Katie to meet him for a minute. She felt a little uncomfortable, having just made an error and not quite sure how he was going to react.

"You got robbed up there, babe. You did everything right, and the shot just didn't go our way. You're doing great. Let's get the next one," Brayden said.

"That's not the husband I've been playing with," Katie thought, "but I sure like this one!" She chimed back, "Thanks, honey. You're serving hot. Let's keep it going."

The game advanced to deuce, add-in, and then the tennis gods were once again with them. He hit another big serve. The opponent struck the ball awkwardly, and it flew into the net. The opponents lost their serve and consequently lost the first set, 6-4. Katie and Brayden walked over to the sidelines and sat on the bench.

"This bench has become common ground, hasn't it?" Brayden observed. "It's where we meet as a team at changeovers. It's where we have a minute to converse and see how we're doing. We can talk strategy adjustments if we want, or just offer encouragement."

"You're right," Katie said thoughtfully.

"So, what do you think we should do differently in the next set?" Brayden asked.

"Let's try to get to the net together more often, hit angle shots to open up the center of the court, and throw some lobs in—particularly to his backhand," said Katie.

"Agreed—good plan. Come on! Skill and will, let's get it done!" said Brayden.

The next set was a nail-biter as both teams played well. The rallies were a grind, and most games progressed to deuce. Katie was playing her best, and they both knew it. He was comfortable seeing that she liked being out there with him, although he still felt a sense of responsibility to help her enjoy the game and maybe get a win together. She made more errors than he did, but that was to be expected. She kept bouncing back. He was able to channel his desire to win into each point, and then, win or lose the point, simply move on to the next one. The set advanced to 6-5, Katie and Brayden in the lead. It was Katie's turn to serve to win the set and the match.

One more time at the changeover, they met on common ground. This time, the common ground was not only the bench, but their collective mindset and mutual support of each other. They found a way to make it work.

The competitive juices began to brew within Brayden. He was a testosterone powerhouse with all turbines rolling on full capacity. However, he was now equipped with a mental filter that enabled him to redirect his desire for victory into his commitment to their game plan. He knew he was a stronger player and would still do his best to get into position to score points, but not at the expense of stupid shots, wasted opportunities, or cutting Katie off from shots that were clearly hers. He was trying his best to make only positive comments and quell his propensity to tell Katie what to do. He took his position at the net, turned, and gave Katie an encouraging wink as if to communicate, "Don't worry. We're going to do this thing."

Katie bounced the ball a few times and thought to herself, "Now I'm serving for the match and need to do my best. I'm confident with Brayden up there at the net. I need to focus on keeping the ball in play and hitting my best shots. Nothing more."

She caught the final bounce in her hand, then tossed the ball and hit her first serve. It was a beauty; she got it to the tee. Brayden picked up on the opponent hitting a weak return and easily moved into position for the put-away—winner!

He trotted over to Katie and said, "Hell of a serve! Keep 'em coming. These guys are nervous, down in the match, down in this game, and really down on each other. Let's keep giving them something to worry about."

"Okay but remember: One point at a time, and play like we're down in the match," said Katie.

Brayden extended his hand for a fist bump. Then, ten minutes later, he ran over to Katie and they did a chest bump. They'd won the game, the set, and the match! They walked together to the net, shook hands with their opponents, and wished them well.

Katie turned and threw her arms around her husband, but before she could say anything he shouted, "You played your heart out, Katie! I'm so proud of you!"

She blushed. "You, too, sweetheart. You're awesome!"

The tournament was over, but their tennis journey had just begun. They walked over to their bench, unzipped their tennis bags, stowed their gear, slung their bags over their shoulders, and began to walk off the court. Katie looked at Brayden. "Guess what?" she said, smiling.

"What's that?" asked Brayden.

"I signed us up for the Mixed 7.5 Tennis Tournament in Palm Springs. We gotta be ready in two weeks. Skill and will – let's go do it!"

Chapter 20

Courtside Coaching: Success at Last
The Authors Offer a Deeper Look

Dr. Clara met Brayden and Katie at the court gate. She peered through the screen and shouted, "You two sure have beaming smiles on your face."

"Yeah, this took a lot of work, but we're starting to figure it out," replied Brayden as he closed the gate behind them.

"Well like a lot of things in life, the things we work the hardest at are the most fulfilling," replied Dr. Clara.

Katie jumped in, "Brayden, I really enjoyed playing with you. For a minute I didn't think I was really playing with my husband."

"You two both stuck to your commitments and stayed upbeat. Those will be two key ingredients to your success," counseled Dr. Clara.

"I felt more in control of my emotions and what to do with them," Brayden replied.

"Brayden, you made me feel great with those positive comments. It made me really want to do my best," said Katie.

"I felt better equipped when things weren't going exactly the way I like. I knew I could channel my emotions, so they didn't manifest themselves into something offensive," said Brayden.

"Well it worked. We both made a few mistakes, but then got over them and moved on to the next point," Katie replied.

"I'm sure you two want to hit the shower and have a nice dinner, so I'll leave you with this. Know what you can realistically expect from each other and stay positive. When you can do this consistently, win or lose, good things will happen. Best wishes to you in the future," Dr. Clara said.

"Thanks Dr. Clara. We will feel better equipped the next time we walk onto the court," said Katie.

***

Recap

Through communication and trial and error, Katie and Brayden weathered the storm. They amended their behavior and aligned mentally. They recognized and accepted each other's strengths and weaknesses. This enabled them to be supportive and tolerant of the other's contributions, both good and not so good.

Brayden had acknowledged to himself that he can't be so rash and react to every impulse if he wants to enjoy playing with Katie. The inner person has to be consistent with the outer person for stability and consistency in character as well as behavior. He learned to let his emotions sift through his mental filter before responding. He was aware of his communication patterns and did his best to send only positive signals.

Katie had learned to set limits, so Brayden couldn't trample all over her—whether he realizes it or not. Eventually, when he slipped, she was less reactive and judgmental, knowing that he was at least trying.

They both realized that learning new behaviors may come quickly for some or take time to develop for others. Both of them came away from the match feeling supported by the other and looking forward to the next time they would play together.

Keys to Success
- *Being accepting of each other's strengths and weaknesses will ease expectations.*
- *Maintain control of your emotions and don't let your actions convey mixed signals.*

- *Set limits so your partner knows what behaviors you can tolerate and which ones you won't.*
- *It takes time to develop new behaviors...stay at it.*

Chapter 21

A Woman's Perspective: Kristi Carter

I wanted to join a country club in 2005 so my husband and I could play tennis and expand our social life. My folks had been members of a club for years where they met new friends and developed many enduring relationships. They've enjoyed an almost family-like bond with these friends. Since we had no children, meeting people our age was difficult. Mike was not as excited to join in the beginning. I really wanted to play tennis and meet some nice gals. Eventually, we ended up joining. I was thrilled—Mike and I were on our way to playing tennis together. I took lessons and started playing USTA matches. We established camaraderie with our new friends. It was wonderful; the start of a whole new way of life for us.

Unfortunately, the idea of playing tennis still didn't resonate with Mike. He would play tennis with me only if I begged him. Eventually my persistence, the people, and the enjoyment of the game won him over. He has always been a great athlete, so tennis seemed to come easy for him. During our first year, I played better and beat him during our practices. However, Mike started to really like playing. He started going to the men's drop-in on Saturdays and playing in practices a couple times per week. He also started playing in USTA matches and winning! He went from a 3.0 to a 4.0 in a matter of 16 months. He turned into a tennis monster! We began playing mixed doubles with our new friends and eventually going to USTA mixed matches.

During our practices or playing tennis with our friends, Mike took it upon himself to be my coach, much like the way Brayden was coaching Katie. He was telling me how to play tennis! Mind you, I started playing a year before he did. I had taken dozens of clinics and lessons. Mike, who had not taken any instruction, was telling me what to do! I couldn't believe it. I have seen similar behavior with other husbands and their wives. This is exactly what Brayden did to upset Katie. When Mike started telling me how to play on the courts, my confidence began to wane. I became frustrated not only because I wanted to just play enjoyable tennis with my husband, but because he was so critical of my tennis abilities. The dream I had about us playing tennis together became a time of anxiety, frustration, and, quite frankly, a nightmare. We were frustrated with each other. I thought that he was putting too much emotion into this "fun" game. I am a competitive person. I wanted to win too, but I wanted to have fun as well. With this type of play at a country club, and with people in their 40's and 50's, I wanted passive competition and just plain, old-fashioned fun.

Playing with Mike in his "competitive" mode was really hard. He would take the ball out of the air right in front of me, tell me where to stand, roll his eyes when I hit into the net, etc. He would slump and drudge, sending a message of defeat. These verbal and physical gestures conveyed messages that made me feel bad. I didn't want to disappoint my partner, but I would end up getting mad and just wanting the game to end. Despite this, I still wanted to be able to play together. That was the whole point of our joining the club in the first place. I envisioned us playing together well into our later years.

We started playing USTA Mixed Doubles after a few years of consistent tennis together. During our practices, Mike was still hogging the ball, telling me what to do, and being super-aggressive. On the upside, he did help me with a few things, like telling me to go up to the net when one of us hit the ball to the opponents' backline. I appreciated some of his coaching, but not all of it. I had to develop an attitude of mental toughness in order to play tennis with my husband. I also had to fight back. I would tell him, "I promise you I will do worse when you talk to me like that." I set boundaries. After a dozen such comments, Mike started realizing that he would get a better player out of me by sending encouraging words rather than derogatory messages to me, his partner in life and on the court.

This is when the idea of writing this book first began to germinate. We had been playing with a dozen couples over the years. Some of them loved playing tennis together and did quite well in their games. But most had a very difficult time playing with their spouse. One partner often seemed to think he or she was better and knew more than the other. Generally, it was the husband, but I shouldn't say this aggressive behavior was always on the part of the man. There were a few instances where the woman would be the aggressor, telling the man what to do, how to play etc. One time I heard a woman screaming at her sweet husband from four courts away. He didn't hit the ball correctly so she 'ripped him a new one' right in front of their opponents. And this was just a practice match! Some of the women can be vicious.

After a few years of playing for fun and in the USTA matches, tennis became more familiar to us. As we matured in our tennis endeavors, we started focusing on really playing together for the joy of being together. Some of our close friends have lost their spouses to illness. When couples like us see that happening around them, they begin to value their own spouse more. They begin to realize that the game of tennis is not about winning at any cost but being able to play together to enhance their relationship, enjoy their partner, and to be healthy. It just isn't worth being upset with each other.

Mike encourages me on the court these days. He is not as intense, and we have a much better time playing together. We even look forward to it. The people we play with are more relaxed as well. When couples are upset with each other on the court, the opponents feel the tension and become uncomfortable too. Every once in a while, Mike still rolls his eyes when I hit into the net, but I just shrug it off and figure 'progress before perfection.' I've become a better player in the last few years, and Mike and I are better players together now because of the time and effort we have taken to learn how to play tennis as a couple. We have learned that encouragement goes a long way in helping your partner be better on the tennis courts and in life.

Chapter 22

The Keys to Success

Mixed troubles? No way! A little time and effort invested in learning to play mixed doubles together will yield rewarding results. We've summarized for you the ten keys that can help:

The first step is to *agree about what you hope to accomplish by playing together*. Well in advance of your match and away from the courts, couples should talk about their objectives. Do you want to win, just have fun, or both? From a relationship standpoint, what outcome would make it a success? Are you participating in a social match, or is it something more competitive?

The two behaviors that are essential are being positive and being supportive, no matter what. These behaviors work wonders under all environments, whether you are winning or losing, stressed or unstressed, happy or disgusted with your partner.

Couples need to *recognize that changing behavior takes real commitment*. Behaviors do not simply change overnight. It isn't easy. The pressure and the heat of competition creates a stressful environment. Strange as it sounds, having a session on the courts, like Bart and Jeanne, in which couples *practice being supportive and positive*, can make all the difference. Give it a try.

Have a strategy for your match. You can reduce some of the stress and add enjoyment to your play by talking in advance about your strategy for the match. Many important decisions about your game plan should be determined before the first serve.

Understand your partner's motivations for the match. Take a minute to think about things from your partner's perspective. No doubt you know him or her well enough. Understanding your partner's motivations will help you endure any misbehaviors—be they verbal or with body language—in a way that is not as hurtful.

Know what you can expect from your partner. Know the abilities of your partner and don't expect your partner to exceed them. Unmet expectations lead to resentments and disappointments. Your partner may give 100%, but 100% from a 3.5 player is not the same as 100% from a 4.5 player. Believe your partner is trying his or her best and stay focused on doing *your best.* Katie and Brayden weathered the storm and found common ground. They were accepting of each other's strengths and weaknesses. This enabled them to be supportive and tolerant of each other's play, both good and not so good.

Have a 'reset' button. Have an honest conversation and discuss how you'll handle tense situations, so they don't escalate into personal conflict. Cultivating coping techniques is a good way to balance stress levels so that they don't inhibit your performance. Develop your own "rules of engagement" to defuse hostile exchanges between you and your partner. Use a saying or a signal that says, "No big deal. Let's get back to enjoying the game." Peter and Stacey chose 'Scottsdale' as their reset button, and when used, it put things in perspective.

Realize heat of the moment comments are just that. Despite best efforts, moments will inevitably arise in which emotions get the best of you or your partner. It's always better to recognize that it is more the heat of the moment than your partner's true character. Try to respond in ways that support your partner rather than escalate tension.

Know when to be competitive and when to back off. You don't need to be competitive all the time. Monitor yourself and keep the big picture in perspective. Is this a social, practice, or league match? When in a low-key social match, back off on the pressure you put on your performance. The lack of pressure and tension will result in a better experience.

Build up; don't tear down. Players need reassurance when they're playing well, as well as when they're not. A little assurance that things will be all right can go a long way. Provide encouragement.

Chapter 23

A Pro's Thoughts

We have the pleasure of knowing tennis professional Nino Louarsabishvili. She was born and raised in Georgia, Russia. Growing up as a young girl in the Soviet Union she was faced with the pre-conceived notion of becoming a pianist or a gymnast, neither of which interested her. Fortunately, for many of us whom have been coached by her, at the age of six she decided to pick up a tennis racquet.

Nino enrolled in a tennis academy and began to learn to play tennis. Born with a competitive spirit she worked diligently to perfect her game. Her efforts paid off. Nino became the number one 10-year-old player in the Soviet Union. In 1993/1994 she became the world's top-ranked Junior Player. She became a Professional tennis Player in 1992. During her professional career she won six singles titles and 7 doubles' titles. She represented her country playing in the both the Fed-Cup and the Davis Cup.

Nino retired from the Pro Circuit after a debilitating injury and moved on to a coaching and teaching career in 2000. She currently is the Director of Tennis at Round Hill Country Club.

We had the pleasure to speak with Nino about married couples mixed doubles. Here's what she had to offer.

"The key is to remember that it's a partnership on the court too. Tennis is a mental game. You should always be pumping each other up. Find ways that work for you to provide encouragement, like high fiving. Different approaches work for each couple, so find one that's encouraging for you."

Here are questions we served up to Nino and her returns.

What do you like about playing doubles?

"Well for starters it's a lot less running! You're on a team and it's social. I enjoy the interactions. My partners and I know what our strengths are and set ourselves up to strategically play to them. We analyze our opponents and work quickly to ascertain their weaknesses. Then we capitalize on them. It's important that you and your partner also know your weaknesses. When you know this, you can strive to protect each other by court position or shot selections."

How can couples deal with the pressure of competition?

"Start by preparing for the match. Hit balls together with your friends or teammates. Think about the process as your match develops, adjust your game plan accordingly. Focus on one point at a time, not the end of the match.

Remember that in a recreational setting no one puts pressure on you except yourself. Some players tend to judge their self-value by their tennis rating. Pride and ego enter the equation. This leads to the self-inflicted pressure that builds within. Perhaps a better approach is to be glad you're on a team and focus on trying your best. Recognize your weaknesses and play in your position of strength.

Each player needs to just understand that their partner is doing their best for today. It may not be as good as it was in the last match, or the next one, but for today it's the best they have."

There's a saying in sports, "play smarter not harder." What does that mean to you?

"It means once a game is underway, as well as during the

match have check points to take a step back, take a deep breath, and focus on what's happening on the court. This is advisable when the momentum changes, which it often does. Resist overplaying in these moments. Overplaying can cause a player to miss shots they normally make. Keep things simple on the court."

What can couples do to stay focused during a match?

"Staying focused during a match is something all amateur players need to work on. The best tip I can give you is that when you practice, and when you work drills practice concentrating on the moment as well. Many players don't do this. They're distracted by sounds and movement around them. Find a way that works for you to get into the zone. Think it's only you and your partner, your opponents, the ball, and the court that are in the moment. It's the end of points in games or sets that matter the most. Don't look around before the next point starts. Stay in your zone. Focus on the score and what you and your partner need to do.

I think, "I want to be the best at whatever I'm doing" whether it's on or off the courts. When I'm on the court I want to do my best. I've learned that "best" is relative, meaning my best today might not be as good as yesterday, but it might be better than tomorrow. It's just what shows up in me in the moment. That doesn't mean I don't keep trying, I always give 100%. However, 100% of good is not the same as 100% of great. Couples should be aware of this.

The best thing for couples is more than winning or losing. It's the appreciating the time you've made to play together and that you have this nice opportunity. Couples can appreciate that tennis is one more thing they have in common. You have a mutual skill that you've both learned together and can share together."

Final thoughts

"Couples should think about why they're playing together. They have so many options on how to spend their free time. Tennis is a great game they can enjoy together. There are not very many other sports that offer this opportunity. There should be no expectations regarding each other's play. Just know your partner is doing their best. Remember, Einstein had a saying, "expectation is the root of all headaches."

Lastly, go to play because you want to win, not because you expect to win."

Chapter 24

What is happening Beneath the Surface? The Five C's

Let's go deeper and explore the interactions that unfold between a couple while they're playing tennis together. We talked with a number of relationship experts and other professionals to try to get a picture of what takes place beneath the surface. Our findings are distilled into five categories, which we term the Five C's: Cranium, Chemistry, Competition, Communication, and Character.

***

Let's start with Cranium.

Generally speaking, men and women have different modes of processing their feelings. They are wired differently. When a woman is emotionally upset, she often seeks a *social* outlet, such as calling a friend on the phone to discuss the matter or to vent her feelings. A man, on the other hand, may often find a *physical* outlet for anger or frustration.

In tennis, a man may react to a bad game with anger and frustration, cursing or damaging his own tennis racquet. A woman, even if equally angry, might react to a bad tennis experience by showing emotional withdrawal, walking out, giving the cold shoulder, or phoning her social support network.

The point is, during a time of stress in a mixed doubles match, women and men are not particularly well prepared to provide the type of support the other needs.

Understanding what makes your partner tick will foster a

better mental attitude, thus a better time together. Try to keep in mind your partner's mindset. You most likely know your spouses's mindset better than anyone else. The intimacy that you share can be an advantage in helping you to keep some perspective about your partner's behavior during stressful times in your matches.

Do you know the number one reason that children over 13 give for quitting league sports? It's pretty simple: Sports stop being fun. The pressure to win increases, and the fear of losing begins to take over. (Source: *National Alliance of Youth Sports)*

Kids are usually into sports for the fun, the excitement, the participation, being with friends, and learning new skills.[2] Why shouldn't it be that way for adults?

Here are a few tips to help develop a mindset that will improve your tennis experience:

Remember why you play tennis in the first place. It should be for social interaction, recreation, and fun, in addition to winning. When too much emphasis is placed on winning or rankings, the fun erodes.

Embrace the core definition of team competition—to strive together.

The little things really do count—look for things in your play or partner's game to feel good about. "Equal" does not have to mean "the same." Accept and respect your differences.

Don't use the excuse "being competitive is just my nature." Allow your better nature to show on the court.

"The mark of great sportsmen is not how good they are at their best, but how good they are at their worst." -Martina Navratilova

Be more considerate than competitive—let your personal success be based on your own play and skill as a partner. Empower your partner to do his or her best and you'll personally win by doing just that.

Alter your mindset by asking yourself at the end of a match, "Did we have fun?" before you ask, "Did we win?"

***

Let's move on to Chemistry.

Keep in mind "chemical balance." Competition increases adrenaline. A little adrenaline can get players on their game. When adrenaline increases, men typically feel more aggressive whereas women typically react somewhat differently — their desire to do their best increases. Your emotions on the court are often a direct result of the amount of adrenaline pumping through your body. However, the flames of adrenaline can quickly combust into a raging fire if players do not monitor themselves, their emotions, and their court etiquette.

What about other hormones? Men typically have more testosterone coursing through their veins, which drives them toward valuing winning and competing. They may grow up playing competitive sports, encouraged to succeed in all walks of personal and professional life. Testosterone levels tend to rise before a match. In males, the relationship between testosterone and the desire for dominance is reciprocal. Not only does testosterone affect dominance, but dominance in competition affects testosterone levels. When a male begins to see his dominance drifting away, for example losing in a mixed doubles match, he may feel anger or frustration and a compulsion to critique his partner.

Several studies suggest that individuals with winning *attitudes* enjoy an increase in testosterone levels, at least temporarily, compared to those without such an attitude. One group of researchers measured testosterone levels in six male college tennis players and found that levels began to rise in all of them before their matches, apparently in anticipation of competition. The surprise came after the fact: The testosterone levels of those who won their matches remained high, while the testosterone levels of those who lost plummeted[3].

We've all heard about the "home court advantage." There is scientific evidence that differential performance in competitive meetings when playing at home may to some extent be attributed to testosterone. Some have proposed that rising testosterone levels are related to expressions of dominance, especially in face-to-face encounters. The pre-competition rise before home games is often greater than that experienced during away games and may make the player more willing to take risks, improve reaction time, enhance certain aspects of spatial ability, and increase the metabolic rate of muscles. It is hypothesized that these represent adaptive responses to facilitate the defense of one's territory.

The take-away in this discussion about testosterone is that it affects mental outlook on the court. Women as well as men will experience a rise in testosterone during a match. However, men may be more likely to stress out or allow emotions to get the best of them, whereupon testosterone level may decline.

Stress leads to a rise in cortisol, another hormone, and cortisol can affect the balance of testosterone in your system.

Women on the other hand tend to be more nurturing, empathetic, social, and detail-oriented. Higher levels of the hormone estrogen may have an effect on how they play. They are not always "out for the kill" as men may be.

Here's the point. Chemicals that the body generates—hormones including adrenaline, testosterone, and estrogen—play a role in your attitude. Their effects can lead to combustion between partners. You need to be aware of this and respond in ways that will help your partner.

**

The third 'C' is Competition.

Competition in sports is immediate. Under the pressure of competition, stress creeps into our bodies. It's the body's mechanism, according to Psychology Today, for preparing itself to meet a tough situation with focus, strength, stamina, and heightened alertness. A little stress can be helpful.

At an optimal level of stress, you have the benefits of an alert mind and activation that improves performance[5]. However, when you are on the tennis court and trying to win, you can't take a breather, re-group, and talk about it later. This immediacy is a major factor in leading to combustibility between partners. Immediacy also leads to more stress. Unchecked, positive stress can morph into distress, a bad type of stress that can exhaust your determination, patience, energy, and communication.

Players can put themselves under a lot of pressure in a tennis match. Most of the time it comes from an innate desire to win or to not let down a partner. Some tennis players are especially hard on themselves[6]. Whatever the cause, the pressure of competition can stress you to the point where you don't know how to have fun anymore.

Stress plays an important role. The circumstances that enable stress are called **stressors**[7], and they cover a whole range of situations—everything from a life-threatening experience to serving for that big match point. Stress can be a response to change or anticipation of something that's about to happen—good or bad, win or lose. People can feel stress over positive challenges, like closing that key account at work, as well as negative ones, like bouncing a check.

In formal terms, there are two types of stress, distress and eustress[8].

Distress is a negative type of stress that develops when beneficial stress begins to erode. Continuous struggling with too much stress can exhaust your energy and drive. It will affect your game as you lose focus and determination. Coping with stress is an important aspect of performance. Whether it is during the tense moments of a championship game or in the midst of that feared public speaking engagement, stress affects your performance.

Eustress[9] is the good type of stress that stems from the challenge of taking part in something that you enjoy but have to work hard for, such as a promotion at work or hosting a successful party. In the word *eustress* the prefix *eu-* derives from the Greek word meaning either "well" or "good."[10] Attached to the word *stress* it literally means "good stress."

Eustress invigorates you, providing a healthy stimulus for any assignment you accept[11]. Many times, stressful events push us to perform to higher levels and excel. This is eustress, and this is the type of stress you and your partner want to have in your court. The choice is really all in the mind.

What are the circumstances that lead to eustress or distress? This depends on a couple of factors, both of which are under your control:

Your personal response to the motivation for the tennis match. Fun? Compete well? Win?

How in control of the situation do you feel? To what extent can you influence the outcome?

When we allow the perceived pressure of a match to erode our eustress, tension begins to build. The enjoyment and challenge of the match deteriorates. Soon limits are crossed, and personal boundaries break down. There seems to be no relief, no end in sight. This is the kind of stress[12] with which most of us are familiar. It is the kind of stress that leads to poor decision-making, temper tantrums, and poor play.

The key to handling the stress of competition is not to try to eliminate it altogether, but to manage it[13]. Stress during sports, as in anything else in life, may be acute, episodic, or chronic. Primarily in sports, it is episodic, whether during a competitive match between friends or a championship game. Developing coping techniques is the most crucial element in balancing stress levels so that they optimize instead of inhibit performance levels. Relaxation, visualization/imagery, self-talk, goal-setting, motivation, and video review are all examples of systems that can be used by athletes. Having realistic expectations of your game *and* your partner's game goes a long way as well.

In the heat of competition, your partner can cause you distress through word or action. Players must enforce limits on their partner's behavior early on before distress builds up to an emotional explosion, and someone walks off the court. If a player puts down his or her partner—even just mildly—the partner needs to call him or her on it rather than brush it off. When boundaries and limits are addressed early on, the wounds heal much faster. Burying hurt and resentment builds to quite a toxic mess. We have to keep each other in line.

Competition can be a game changer in your relationship as well as a game changer on the court. For some, the goal of winning is like a light switch, either on or off. Here are a few tips to keep things in perspective:

Know when it's time to be competitive. Monitor yourself and keep the big picture in perspective: Is winning as important as keeping your relationship intact?

Know the ability of your partner. Don't expect him or her to exceed it. Unrealistic expectations may lead to resentment and disappointment.

***

Our next 'C' is Communication.

Many of the experts we consulted have found consistent communication misalignment between men and women. When a man puts down his spouse in the heat of the moment, he often attributes it to a slip of the tongue in the stress of the match. But the woman often thinks that her man truly feels that way underneath, and that the pressure of the match revealed what he believes but doesn't verbalize at home. The woman then questions her partner's true feelings, which creates insecurity in the relationship. Men tend to go on with life and forget the comment.

Women tend to go on with life and never forget the comment.

Whether male or female, do you express negativity, either with words or mannerisms? You may communicate disappointment, anger, or sadness. Your partner is then set on edge, picking up the negative vibes of the communication and not benefiting from the intended "correction." As we all know, it can become downright depressing to receive *or* give negativity. No one wants to be the recipient of constant corrections from a spouse. Although obvious, you should try to communicate without the negative twist.

A mindset of "let's have fun and good things will happen" is contagious as well. Positive thinking will generate a positive attitude: "I have your back whether we win or not." From the mental decision to be positive the feelings will follow.

***

The final 'C' is 'Character.'

One goal of a tennis game, obviously, is to win. If you have the right opportunity and the right set of skills and talents, you can succeed. But winning doesn't need to be the only goal in tennis, and certainly not in mixed doubles. Winning the battle for character is more difficult than winning in tennis. In life, greatness is not seen in trophies or records; it is seen in character. Here's what Chris Evert has to say about this, "If you can react the same way to winning and losing, that's a big accomplishment. That quality is important because it stays with you the rest of your life, and there's going to be a life after tennis that's a lot longer than your tennis life." Wise words from a real champion.

The pressure of competition makes it hard to maintain one's character. Couples want to win, of course, but the pressure of vulnerability, of playing in front of others, exposing oneself to criticism, making an embarrassing move, all heighten the tension. The bar is raised by criticism and humiliation on a bad play. It is easier to blame a partner. Taking charge is an attempt to reduce the building stress and the humiliation of losing. *The problem, however, is that the response a woman seeks when stressed on the court is not the response a man is likely to provide when he is similarly stressed.* And the reverse holds true as well. This is the exact moment when it's so important to maintain character.

Character is your individual combination of qualities that make you a distinct person. Let's take a look at a few qualities that are helpful on the courts.

Thoughtfulness: The match may or may not be going your way. Be cognizant of how your partner is feeling. Thoughtfulness really makes a difference in terms of maintaining a healthy team mindset.

Supportiveness: Support each other when you're going through hard times on the court. Encourage each other to try something new that may turn things around.

Flexibility: You can't always expect to get your way. You should be able to talk things through without either partner getting defensive. A healthy relationship requires that you listen to one another and sometimes give in!

The next time you have a quiet moment of reflection, we challenge you to think about these questions: What is the content of my character? How do I need to conduct myself on the court to maintain my character?

Chapter 25

Behind the Scenes: Excerpts from Interviews with Mixed Doubles Couples

W
e conducted a series of interviews to gain insights from real couples about how they make mixed doubles work, and, in some instances, why they haven't. We think you will both enjoy and learn from these interviews.

***

Ray and Janet – Alamo, California

Tell us about playing tennis together?

Ray and Janet: We met playing mixed doubles together 35 years ago at the San Francisco Racquet Club. The venue was for single people to show up and form teams to play mixed doubles…a real mixer! We played for an hour and a half. Then we'd go to dinner at someone's home where we'd all bring something or chip in for the costs. We really enjoyed the experience.

Talk to us about some specific examples when you've had an enjoyable experience playing together?

R&J: Getting to meet each other on the courts was a great experience. At the dinners and afterwards, it was very social, and we really enjoyed getting to know each other.

Tell us about a bad or negative experience?

Janet: I get upset with Ray after I've made a good shot. The opponents return it, but then Ray misses his shot when the ball comes back to him, losing the point. It frustrates me because I'm the weaker player and don't hit that many good shots. When I do, I want us to win the point. When we don't due to Ray's error, I give him the evil eye! We've found that if we've had a 'bad day,' it's a good idea to let the other person know before a match starts. Otherwise, it may get projected on the court. Tell your partner beforehand how you're feeling, so words and actions aren't misinterpreted, and potentially ugly flare ups are avoided.

What makes you feel like you'd rather play with another partner other than your spouse?

Janet: I like playing against Ray, so I can get back at him! I can target my shots and make him run or direct balls right at him...nasty!

Ray: I believe I step up my game when playing with a different partner. I strive to do better. I feel more inclined to win with a different partner than just going out to play with Janet.

Ray, what's it like at home after verbally or non-verbally blaming your spouse on the court? How long does this tension between you last once you're off the court?

Ray: It depends how acute the signal is indicating how abusive the comment is. The tension is short-lived because we always go out to lunch, and I have a couple of beers. Then things just seem right again. However, during the match if something comes up, I can't put it out of my head. It sticks with me until after the match. When something is stuck in my head, it does affect my tennis performance.

How long does this tension between you last once you're off the court?

R&J: Not long. We only play 6 times a year together at this stage of the game, and it's social tennis.

Ray: I will play with my wife 6 times per year (lunch and beer to follow.

What triggers the ensuing argument?

R&J: Possibly backed up resentment or frustration...usually not major. Also, each of us knows how to push the other person's button to tick them off. We may push it during a frustrating game or series of bad points.

Why do you feel you can critique, coach, or yell at your spouse but not an alternative partner?

R&J: We're emotionally attached to each other. There are not many inhibitions to say what's on our minds...so we do!

When you play with another partner, what is it that makes you feel you need to be cordial with them, as opposed to playing with your spouse where perhaps you're different?

Ray: I don't have to go home with them! I try harder being nice to be nice. Meaning, I'm more tolerant of their mistakes and tend to say more positive and encouraging things during our match.

Janet: More courteous, good manners are a given.

How is it different on the court playing with a partner other than your spouse?

Ray: I feel I raise my game to support my partner. It's not that I don't want to play well with Janet, but I just feel inclined to play my best with a different partner.

Why do you think your spouse offers unsolicited advice during a match?

Ray: I don't mind a suggestion from a stronger player if it's presented in a learning situation. Sometimes it's how you say it. I think sometimes it's like water steaming up in a tea kettle and wanting to come out. There's frustration or junk carrying on from something else, and it just comes out.

There are many couples out there that would like to play tennis together but choose not to. What advice would you offer these people that might lead them to changing their minds?

R&J: Try to make it fun and social. Don't make it competitive. Have lunch afterwards, two beers are good too! Take a lesson together. In the event you do play competitive tennis go overboard to give support to each other. Focusing on supporting and encouraging your partner tends to lift one's play, and the errors aren't as big a deal.

What types of words do you enjoy hearing from your partner when you're playing in a match?

R&J: Only encouraging words like, "nice shot dumpling."

Assuming you've walked off the court with a nice win together, how does it feel?

R&J: Good, any win feels good. Even though it's social and not supposed to be competitive it still feels good to win. It makes us feel like we had a good experience and a nice time together.

Authors note: *Many times throughout our conversation, Ray said, "Doubles is about supporting your partner."*

***

Bob and Marie – Danville, California

Tell us about playing tennis together?

Bob and Marie: We've been playing for 7 years. We try to communicate in a manner that doesn't create conflict.

Talk to us about some specific examples when you've had an enjoyable experience playing together?

B&M: We have a "code system" we've established. It is a signal that says, "You're getting close to crossing a boundary you don't want to!" Our code is for Bob to say, "Nice skirt, honey," and in turn Marie says, "Nice shorts, honey." This helps to keep things light.

What do you think made it an enjoyable experience?

B&M: We complimented and reinforced the good stuff. We liked to hear good things about our play.

What's it like at home after verbally or non-verbally blaming your spouse on the court? How long does this tension between you last once you're off the court?

B&M: We have not had that experience. We have a code word, "black moon," that one of us will say in a heated exchange. Then, we both immediately stop arguing and go to a neutral corner to regain our composure.

How long does this tension between you last once you're off the court?

B&M: We don't feel we have this problem. We've learned through trial and error how to sense we may be going too far and then don't go there.

Why do you feel you can critique, coach, or yell at your spouse but not an alternative partner?

B&M: Familiarity with other.

How has your relationship on the tennis court evolved over time?

Bob: I get satisfaction from seeing how Marie has progressed in her game.

When you play with another partner what is it that makes you feel you need to be cordial with them as opposed to playing with your spouse where perhaps you're different?

B&M: Lack of familiarity with the other person, not knowing them.

How is it different on the court playing with a partner other than your spouse?

Bob: I'm more willing to play my best. I'm not as competitive, more accommodating.

Is it you who won't play with your spouse or your spouse who won't play with you? Why?

Marie: I sense that he wants me to play more like him. He's an "implementer," an idea person, very technical and fastidious. I'm a loose cannon and go by feel. For instance, he needs a recipe to cook or bake something, and I just go by taste.

Why do you think your spouse offers unsolicited advice during a match?

B&M: Competitiveness and ego.

Marie: Bob tells me at the beginning of every point, "I'm back you get the net." I take that as, "don't you think I know that?" The way his mind works is that he mentally resets himself for every point. He's only in the moment of the current point, and then he's on to the next one as if nothing just happened. He wants to be competitive with each point, doing his best, and then onto the next one.

Bob: I don't really care who wins the match, but I want to do my best each point.

Authors Note: *We asked Marie if she heard what Bob said. She said, "Yes." We then asked her if she would feel any different on the court when Bob says, "I'm back you get the net?" She said no, "I'll still take it negatively!" When asked why, Marie said, "Because I just don't like being told what to do…Period!"*

Why do you feel like you can offer unsolicited advice during a tennis match?

Bob: Is there a right way to say something that might help your partner? I'm just trying to help her play better. I don't mean to upset her.

What do you think drives you to feel the need to win and dominate a match?

Bob: I played competitive sports since I was 6 years old. My parents imposed an attitude of succeeding in me. Looking back, I think my childhood experiences, such as striving to win the gold medal at the state fair, instilled competitiveness as well.

There are many couples out there that would like to play tennis together but choose not to. What advice would you offer these people that might lead them to changing their minds?

B&M: Create an environment to help them play with each other and have fun. Keep it light, playing with another couple.

Prior to a match, do you and your spouse discuss strategy and/or the strengths and weaknesses of your opponents? If so, do those discussions add to the enjoyment of the experience?

B&M: No, but we probably should.

***

Craig and Marta – San Ramon, CA

Tell us about playing together?

Craig and Marta: We started playing tennis in college. We enrolled in a tennis class. Marie: When the weather warmed up, he started noticing me when I wore my tennis outfits. We played competitive tennis against each other, and I would always beat him.

Note from the authors: *He confirmed that was true unless it was for money!*

What do you think made playing tennis together an enjoyable experience?

C&M: We made a mind shift away from being overly competitive to committing to having fun. We have found something we like to do and never have to go to the gym.

What makes you feel like you'd rather play with another partner other than your spouse?

C&M: We prefer to play with each other. It took us seven years for us to learn how to play together.

Craig: I learned during those seven years that what I was saying to Marta needed to match what my body language was saying too. Playing well together is a reflection of our relationship and our communication skills.

What would you offer or suggest to other mixed doubles couples to develop a more complimentary game?

C&M: Just play social until you feel more confident, play in tournaments, work on your weaknesses, and maximize your strengths.

How long does the tension last between you once you're off the courts?

C&M: We have a saying, "An equal voice at home equates to

an equal voice on the court." When we communicate openly and stay positive, we don't experience too much tension.

What do you think drives players to feel they need to win and dominate a match?

C&M: We think that it is a cultural derivative. It gives people a sense of identity they may not have. Winning to them compensates for something that may not be working in their lives. It really is an ego thing. We think a good goal is to feel good when you've played your best, regardless of having won or lost the match.

Tell us about a bad or negative experience.

C&M: We haven't had any for a long time. We have a choice on how we spend our free time together, and we like to spend it with each other on the courts.

Craig: Our relationship in tennis has grown over the years. She's fluid and I'm rigid. We have a tennis partnership, and, as the years go by, long after winning or losing, we'll remember how we feel about each other not how much we won or lost.

Any final thoughts you'd like to share?

C&M: Respect the partnership, smile and laugh a lot on the courts, don't take it too seriously, and play mixed tennis as a fun thing (play for fun before winning). It's a priceless way of spending quality time with your spouse. Playing mixed tennis is a good way of meeting people and developing friendships.

***

Colleen and Steve – San Jose, CA

Do you enjoy your time on the court together?

Colleen and Steve: When we were winning, we did. We thought it was great, and in a way, we thought our success on the court was a reflection of our success as a married couple. We thought that all of the effort we put into our relationship in a way led to our success on the court. We felt we had something special that in turn helped to give us an advantage on the court. We had heard so many stories about couples who just couldn't stand to play together, and that made us feel even better about ourselves.

What about when you lost?

C&S: That's the thing. When we first started playing together in matches, we won every time. Then, we lost. What made it worse was that we thought we would win, and in fact we were comfortably ahead at one point. It was devastating. We began to unravel. We called into question all of the good things we thought about ourselves and our relationship.

In the match where it fell apart, I got extremely frustrated and angry when my partner told me to start saving my energy for the next match. I've played enough to know that you can't let up until the match is over. The comments really got under my skin, and things went straight downhill.

How did it affect your willingness to play together?

C&S: Put it this way, before the match was over, I uttered the famous phrase in some anger but mostly frustration, "I will never play with you again!"

Do you take tennis seriously?

C&S: Well, yes. It is part of our lives, and also part of life. When I'm working on things in my personal life, I consciously try to work on those same things when playing tennis. It helps.

Part II:

Strategy and Technique

Chapter 26

Different Strokes for Different Folks

Part I: Basic Mixed Doubles Strategy

Talk about these basic points of strategy *prior* to your match to reduce stress and increase confidence *during* the match. Be happy you're playing *together*, and understand that each of you will be trying their *best*.

Positioning:

Who Plays Where? Put your higher-skilled player on the ad side. Why? Three reasons: 1) More pressure-filled, important points tend to take place on the ad side. 2) The higher-skilled player will be in position to get to and hit overheads when your opponents hit short lobs in the middle part of the court. 3) On deep lobs, your higher-skilled player will have an easier path to the ball and be better positioned to hit an overhead or strong forehand (assuming he or she is right handed).

Up or Back or Both? There are three basic formations in doubles tennis. 1) Two up, where both players are up at the net, 2) one up and one back, where one player is up at the net and the other stays back near the baseline, and 3) two back, where both players remain on the baseline. Positioning up at the net is the most aggressive and offensive positioning. A two-up strategy works well when both players are good volleyers. However, in mixed doubles, a two-up strategy may not be the best one if one or both players are weak at the net. If both players are stronger at the baseline, a better strategy may be to stay back, hit good shots, then attack when an opening develops during the point.

Movement on the Court. You and your partner should agree about how you will shift during points. Most experts recommend that you move in tandem, maintaining a standard distance between one another. Imagine a rope that connects the two of you such that when one player moves to the left, the other is pulled in the same direction. Such movement helps cut down the angles for your opponents and reduces the opportunity for them to hit a shot through your middle.

Who Will Take the Middle Ground? Before the match, agree who will take shots down the middle. Generally, this should be the higher-skilled player, especially if he or she is hitting forehand down the middle.

Opponents:

Play the Lesser-skilled Player - In a competitive match, the lesser-skilled player may be your target. Hit with pace. Hit topspin. The lesser-skilled player may make errors and is less likely to hit a winner at your team.

Put Your Opponents to the Test - Test your opponents for weaknesses in their partnership. Try a shot or two down the middle. If they react in an uncoordinated fashion, you may have the opportunity throughout the match to win points by playing the ball to the space between them.

Bring It - Try to get a feel for how your opponents react to aggressive play. When your team moves towards the net or when you put a little more heat on your shots, how do they react? If you win a point by playing more aggressively, move on to the next point as fast as possible and play that point aggressively as well. Often, you can rattle off a number of points quickly before your opponents know what hit them.

The Net:

Take Your Time - No, you don't have to crash the net together. Allow the game to develop. You don't have to charge the net; one player up and one back is fine unless you are pulled in by a short ball. Serve and volley is best if you can score more points by doing it, otherwise it is "pointless."

Blind Alley - Playing smart doubles is about trying to gain good court position and control of the net. Yet, many recreational doubles players unwittingly hinder their teams by standing near the alley as their partners serve. Although this might prevent you from getting burned down the line, it also makes it more difficult for you to intercept the most common return (the one down the middle), while at the same time making it easier for the returner to execute the crosscourt return. Also, by standing near the alley you leave your serving partner to cover the equivalent of an entire singles court.

The smart choice is to place yourself in the position that increases your chances of having a play on the most common shots. When your partner is serving, stand smack in the middle of the service box. This is the right location because it puts you in good position to volley weak returns, poach, cover lobs, and handle all but the best returns directed down the line[16].

Get the Signal - Poaching on the service return, or just the threat that you may poach, puts significant pressure on the returner. A good strategy is to poach once or twice early in the match on each of your opponents. If you do decide to poach, set up a signaling system in which the net player signals his or her intention to the server.

Pretend Poach - The movement of the server's partner is confusing to the opponents and keeps them guessing where to hit their next return.

Strokes:

Starting the Point When Serving - The strategy for starting the point is simple: Get your first serve in as often as possible. You will be better off taking something off of the first serve and hitting a more controlled serve (similar to a second serve) and getting it in, rather than going for the ace and consistently miss-ing. Why? It has to do with the strategy of the returner. When awaiting a first serve, the returner typically has a defensive mind-set and attempts to simply return the ball and keep it in play. On a second serve, the returner tends to be more offen-sively minded and is likely to hit a return that is more difficult for your team to handle.

Who serves first? The golden rule is that the stronger server always serves first. You want to start a set winning your first game on your own serve.

Placement Before Power - Every good doubles team needs what we call a "closer" in their serving arsenal. Just like on a baseball team's pitching staff, this is the player you can depend on to shut down the other team and hold serve. It would be nice if you could blast 110 m.p.h. aces to win your serve consistently, but it's not a necessity. It's more important to connect on a high percentage of first serves, place them well, and get yourself in excellent volleying position[17].

Return to Sender - It goes without saying that keeping the ball in play when returning serve is job one. Your chances of getting your return past the net player increases if your oppo-nent feels compelled to guard the alley and therefore less able to poach. In practice, there is only one way to keep your oppo-nent anchored: whack a return down the line. The first time you and your partner receive serves that you can handle, take a shot down the alley. Even if your shot misses or your opponent vol-leys it for a winner, it may open the cross court for future service returns.

Be Steady - The lesser-skilled player should play rock-solid positional tennis and not make a lot of unforced errors. Just strive to play steady; try not to attempt shots with a high degree of difficulty. Stay out of no- man's land and either be up near the net or back around the baseline.

Do Much, but Not Too Much - The higher-skilled player's job is to play rock-solid shots but not overplay the court. Try not to go after balls that you cannot put away, as this leaves the court open for winning shots from the other team. Be aggressive in the right measure.

Middle - Aim for the net strap; it's the lowest part of the net.

Play from a Position of Strength - Cheat to one side to give yourself a better opportunity to hit your best shot. For instance, if your best shot is your forehand, position yourself to the left (if you are right-handed).

Lobby for the Lob - The lob is an especially important shot in doubles. A well hit offensive lob can be a winner, and a defensive lob will force your opponents back from the net and prevent them from maintaining aggressive court positioning. When possible, try to lob over your opponent's back hand, as this will maximize the degree of difficulty for their return play. Use the lob early to let your opponents know that when they rush the net, it can be at their peril!

***

Part II: Let's Fix This...Your Personal Stroke Diagnostic Kit

Ask yourself these questions:

Are you giving your opponent too many free points?

Usually errors outnumber winners. To advance in a match, a smart strategy is to focus on committing fewer errors rather than trying to hit winners. Remember the acronym "BIP" which means keep the "BALL IN PLAY." Aim for the strap. It's the lowest part of the net.

Be aware of the differences between power and control. When you hit hard, you may give up some control. This increases your odds of making an unforced error. Striking the ball softer may allow you to have better control of shots and lead to a reduction in errors. Focus on hitting your shots high over the net and away from the net-person's reach.

Knowing where to place the ball is often a better weapon than trying to hit powerful winners. Tennis can be a game of inches; inches that determine whether your ball is in or out; inches that determine whether the point goes to you or your opponent. Controlling the ball is a better approach than crushing the ball. Don't be caught saying, "Missed it by this much!" Remember the acronym "POP" which stands for "PLACEMENT OVER POWER." Do this and score more points. Finding the open court is preferable to drilling an opponent.

Are you working your game plan?

Resolve and mental strength can often surmount physical or mechanical weaknesses. Skill and will can get it done! A player that is not as strong as an opponent can win by using more effective strategies, superior anticipation, and more sustained concentration[18]. Think of these two words, "BOUNCE – STRIKE," meaning stay completely focused on the tennis ball. Watch the opponent strike the ball, watch the ball bounce, keep your eyes focused on the ball as you swing, then start the process over again, "BOUNCE – STRIKE."

Pressure is part of a competitive game. Concentrate on the game plan and stay focused on one point at a time. Pressure is normal in a match so learn to work with it. Here are some tips to help during these moments:

"Champions take chances and pressure is a privilege." Billie Jean King (4)

An alarm should go off in your head at 30-30. The next point is critical. You will be either a point away from losing or winning the game. Stop and talk to your partner.

Based on the set score by the fourth game in that set, you should either have to change strategies (because you're losing) or stay the course (because you're on serve or winning). Don't wait until after you lose a set to make a change in strategy.

How are you serving, and how's your return of serve?

My Serve? It's a high-value stroke and an important weapon in my match. It's probably my least practiced stroke. If my opponent breaks me once, that's all she may need to do to win the set. Are my serves going into the net or going long? Are my crushing serves, or "bulls-eye" placement serves, good offensive strokes, or do I need to hit second serves until my serve comes around? My serve should dictate how the rest of the point unfolds.

Toss the ball as high as your extended arm and racquet to the 1:00 p.m. position if you are right handed, and 11:00 a.m. if you're a lefty. Keep your eyes so focused on the ball that you can read the brand and number. This will help to keep your head up. Remember to use a throwing motion similar to a baseball player or quarterback. Maintain a light grip and swing with a loose arm, elbow, and wrist. If your serves are going into the net, you should toss the ball higher. If your serves are going long, you should toss the ball lower.

The return of serve is as important as a strong serve. Correctly executed with a good finish, it can crush your opponent's ability to accomplish a strategic part of his or her game plan which is to stay on serve. The words "READY-READ-REACT" will help you stay mentally and physically prepared to return your opponent's serve, regardless of how big or soft he or she delivers it. READY: Be in the proper spot and angle in relationship to the server. READ: Stay focused on the ball from the moment it leaves the servers hand, strikes his racquet, and travels into your return box. REACT: Split step and execute the proper shot selection.

How well are you executing your strokes?

Every match requires a player to be cognizant of what is and is not working, and to make adjustments. Don't continue to make the same mistakes again and again. Use what is working or try something different. Use the phrase, "RACQUET-FEET-FOLLOW THROUGH" to remind yourself to take your racquet back early, move your feet into proper position in relationship to the ball, and finish high following through at shoulder level. Be sure your feet are getting into position before your racquet when hitting a volley. Often times when a player is going for a ball, the player will hit the ball before setting up, which generally leads to an error. Get your feet there first, set-up, and then hit the ball.

Appropriate shot selection

Choose the right shot for the right situation. Trying to hit winners from a defensive position (when off balance, deep behind the baseline, or out of position) is the main source of unnecessary errors. Be patient and hit solid well-placed shots from strong court positions. It's instrumental to winning the match. Limit volleys to high-odd net shots. Use the phrase, "HOLD ON, REACH OUT," and visualize the number "7." You need to be patient. Anticipate the correct moment to engage the volley. Don't take a back-swing but step towards the ball. Time the stroke to contact the ball in front of your body and thrust the racquet forward with the head up as if to "punch" the ball. The follow-through on the volley is short but definite. This movement looks like a "7." "HOLD ON, REACH OUT."

***

Part III: Mindset of the Higher-skilled Player

In a marriage or relationship, there are three elements always in play: You, your spouse or significant other, and the convergence of these two-independent people as a couple. This is represented by the center circle. You can see the blending or merging where two people are unified.

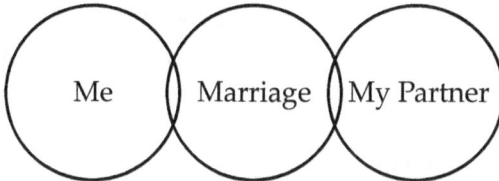

Me   Marriage   My Partner

Let's take a look at how these circles may shift in a match. Because you are the higher-skilled player on your mixed doubles team, it comes with responsibilities. The relationship dynamics are not quite the same. There is a shift in the forces at work. So, your circle of influence bears greater weight, as noted by the larger circle in the diagram.

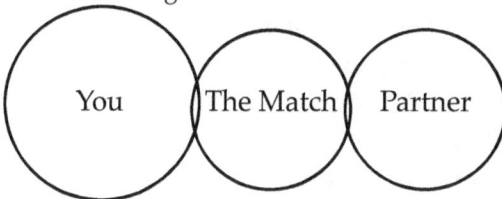

You   The Match   Partner

"For better or for worse" … it applies to tennis too. Whether you're the guy or gal, you have an obligation to help your spouse win and/or enjoy your mutual tennis experience. You're the one who needs to be the "captain of the ship" and navigate your team through both smooth and rough waters. Oftentimes, the smooth waters or easier matches don't require much strategy, just a lot of positive chatter between you and your partner. It's the rough waters and treacherous conditions that should bring out the best in your skill, will, leadership, and strategic capabilities.

Get Behind the Eyes of your Partner

In every match you play, the lesser-skilled partner is always looking up to you to carry the moment and win points. That's very important. Read it again. The lesser-skilled partner knows they're not as consistent. They already feel anxious about the match. They don't want to blow it, and they don't want to let you down. A partner can only deliver to the best of their abilities. They're looking up to you to guide the team and stay positive. You have a responsibility to make sure your partner has the best experience a partner can have; winning or getting pummeled!

One Point at a Time

There's no better saying in tennis than, "Let's get one point at a time." The thought here is to be fully engaged in the point, and then move on regardless of the outcome. You're into the moment of trading strokes with your opponent, and then it's done; the point is over. No matter what occurred, there's nothing you can do about it. After a point ends, ask yourself how you won the point or how you lost the point. Concentrating on the next shot and simply playing one point at a time are the easiest ways to stay optimistic during a match. Don't carry frustration into the next point or series of points. It only makes matters worse for you and your partner.

Tip: There are three words you can go to when things aren't quite going your way: "Only the ball." It remedies, at least for the moment, most of the big snags. Whether you're upset, angry, nervous, or frustrated, say these three words, "only the ball," to block out negative thoughts and refocus your attention.

Be a Pinball Machine

Remember, as the net person, you are in the power seat. You can produce two types of outcomes. You can influence intangible results by distracting your opponents, which may cause them to make errors, or by direct results, which is to say, by scoring points with your racquet. You're a valuable person in any point. What you do is vital to the outcome of the match. You're the stronger player and may be able to dictate how points go. When you're at the net, bounce around, fake poach, poach, and keep moving. Oftentimes, when weaker players are hitting, they go to the lob. Being at the net should give you fertile ground to put balls away. It's a very effective tactic in mixed doubles.

The relationship between you and your partner (the server) is much like that of a quarterback to his wide receiver in football. The quarterback calls the plays because he is in a better position to observe the goings-on in the field. The net person is in a similar position to the quarterback because he can clearly see the opponent's side of the court. The server is occupied concentrating on delivering the best possible serve. You can take some of that pressure off by being a good net person and checking in with your partner.

If you observe that your opponents are frequently hitting up the middle, try to intercept one of the balls and cut off the shot. Make the returner-of-serve think about what to do next. Poach a few times, even if you miss. Once you've done that, throw in some pretend poaches. Doing so may keep the returner second-guessing himself.

Try to read your opponents. Observe how they move after they hit a shot. Do they move in for a volley or lay back for your returns? Watch their eyes. They'll telegraph to you where the shot is going. Do your best to confuse and surprise them. Try to hit your shots into the open court.

Read Between the Lines

Determine early on in the match who the lesser-skilled player is on the opposite side of the net. Then, employ a little counter-intelligence. Most players tend to think that they should just direct every ball to the lesser-skilled player. A better plan may be to look for the open court and direct your shots there. When you hit at a lesser-skilled player, the ball may come back. When you read between the lines and hit to the open court, it's not likely the ball will be traveling back. Generally speaking, if one of the players is weaker than the other, then it usually holds true that

that this person will be out of position. This will give you opportunities to score points.

When You Receive

Know your game plan before it's your team's turn to receive.
When you are returning, try to hit sharp angle shots into the
service box. This will either score points for you or pull the
server out of position, thus opening up the court. Another effective return is to hit a high deep ball with lots of topspin. This
pushes the server back and, many times, makes a hard shot to
return. In both cases, these shots often produce a weak return
that your partner can put away at the net. Always mix up your
returns to keep the opponents guessing what you'll do next.

Get a read on what the opposing net person is doing. Does
he or she go for the poach repeatedly? Do they frequently throw
in fake poaches to distract you? You have a couple of counter-
assault weapons you can deploy. You can crack a few up the line
to make them think twice about how much he or she poaches,
and you can hit lobs for them to chase down and think about.
Stay in touch with your partner to communicate what you plan
to do.

A crucial skill to master as the net person is not with your
racquet. It's with your eyes. Constantly focus on the eyes of the
opposing team. Their eyes will telegraph to you everything you
need to know. This includes where your partner's shot is going.
The opponents need to look, and move to where the ball is
going, and then look (telegraph) to where they hit the ball.

*Tip - You should never look back to watch your partner hit the ball.
Always stay focused on your opponents and what they're doing. Their
eyes, shot set-up, and body language are a good intelligence gathering
system to help you get into position to intercept their returns and
wreak havoc.*

Adapting to Misfortune

Tennis is a game of overcoming opposition as every part of the game presents demanding contests every step of the way. During a competitive tennis match, the challenges your match presents are an unavoidable circumstance. The circumstances can come from the team on the other side of the net, the crowd watching your match, the weather, and even your mind.

Professional athletes have learned to deal with these challenges by developing a stronger mental tennis mindset. In every great venture in life, overcoming obstacles finds its way into the situation. Overcoming misfortune is a test of a player's mental fortitude. Players must strengthen their minds to deal with uncomfortable situations. If you're the better skilled player on your team, you should be mentally stronger as well.

Challenge Yourself – Your Private Game

Challenge yourself to play the best tennis you can. You're actually playing in two matches; one with your partner, and, the other is a private game within yourself. It's against yourself. You need to know you're hitting your best shots, serving well, and not make many errors. If you feel like you've accomplished this at the end of the match, regardless of the outcome, it's a win for you.

So You Lose.............So what!

What will be different tomorrow....win or lose? Answer? Nothing. You still have to go to work. The sun still rises in the morning and sets in the evening. You still need to pay your mortgage. The point is life goes on. The match isn't a life game changer. It's supposed to be fun. Sure it would be nice to win but as long as we tried to play our best and still lost, it's a win.

Part IV: If you're the Less Skilled Player: What You Can Do to Contribute More Points

Your goal is to lose fewer points while winning more points. That's why you so often hear the phrase, "Let's keep the ball in play." Let the other team make the mistakes.

Keep in mind that every error a tennis player commits is a free-point for the team on the other side of the net. How many times in a Grand Slam Tournament have you seen a close match, a real nail-biter, *lost* because the ball was dumped into the net or hit out of play? We've all done it......*error!* The simple premise is to commit fewer errors and make fewer mistakes than your opponent. Mentally prepare yourself by knowing what your best shots are and then hit them when the opportunity arises... ....*utilize your skills where they're the best.* Conversely know what your weaknesses are and don't hit those shots. *When you pay attention to what you can't do, you pay attention to what you can do.*

Play in *control,* be *consistent,* and good things will happen. Think about the skier skiing out of control, hot dogging it, and ending up in a tree. He was skiing beyond his skill level and ultimately wiped out. The same is true in tennis. Play within your limits and keep the ball in play. This doesn't mean letting up – it mean hitting solid, high percentage shots. This is a good way to support your partner because either the other team is going to make an error or your partner will be in position to hit a winner or put-away and........ you've won a point! When you're focused on hitting only your *best high odds* shots, it helps put your partner in position to hit their *best shots* too. *Now you've played to your teams' strength.*

Always Be Talking

Be the one to start communicating .....Get it going – keep it going. We've already discussed how important communication can influence the outcome of your match. This communication can sometimes be the difference between winning and losing a match. Teamwork breaks down when there's a lack of communication, and the breakdown of team work in mixed doubles can leave your game in shambles. Good communication is critical for two players to work together during a match.

Mix Up Your Groundstrokes

You can catch your opponent off guard with a lob or drop shot. Then, attack with your strong shot; that forehand, approach shot or volley that's a solid shot for you or your partner. Do not take unnecessary risks that may produce unnecessary errors and lose a point; play to stay in the point until that opportunity arises to win a point. Those who are less skilled often try to hit offensive shots from court locations where they should hit defensive shots. These are higher odds shots to help your team stay in the point.

Take Advantage of Your Opponents' Weakness

Look for weaknesses in your opponents during warm-ups. Often you can ascertain what their weaknesses are and use them to your advantage during the match.

Stay in the Point

Don't be in a hurry to end the point quickly unless you have a clear 100% for sure shot at making the point. It would be advisable to keep the ball in play with your shots. Stay in the point. This will allow your partner to get into position for a put away, or, in the ensuing exchange of shots, your opponent may make an error.

Down the Middle Solves the Riddle

Hit straight down the middle to take the angles away from your opponent. This often catches your opponents off-guard and can create confusion as to who should hit the ball. How often have you heard, "I thought that you were going to hit that ball?"

When You are Serving

In doubles, the server normally stands between the doubles sideline and the center. You can keep the receiver guessing as to what serve is coming by changing your serving locations every now and then. This way you won't telegraph to your opponent where you intend to serve the ball.

Make Your First Serve Count

It goes without saying that it is a big advantage to get your first serve in. It is more difficult to return a serve (especially the first serve) in tennis doubles than in tennis singles because of the server's partner attempts to cut shots off. Thus, for the server's team side, one of the best tennis doubles approach to winning points is to get the first serve in. This may set up your partner for a put-away, force your opponent to hit a weak return, or cause an unforced error. The server's team has a better chance of winning if they achieve high percentage of good first serves.

Poaching Strategy

From the name itself, the server's partner pretends to poach by moving early (earlier than when you actually do poach) for the opponents to see him/her moving (but only to move back to cover the doubles alley.) You're simply making a strong head fake or, taking a step to the left or right. Then get back into position. When you're at the net, your strategy should be to keep your opponents guessing as to where their next return should go. Keep them confused so they don't know what you'll do as the net person and don't know where the server will place the ball.....in other words confuse your opponent without taking any chances.

These strategies all work primarily because the focus is on keeping the ball in play. This puts pressure on your opponent as they try to end the point quickly which could lead to unforced errors. It also allows your partner to work into position to put the ball away. Your efforts will be rewarded; *effort is a weapon.* Stay in the point, and you'll reap the returns.

Chapter 27

Closing Note

One of the rewards of researching and writing this book was improving on-court relationships with our wives. Like the fictitious couples in our stories, all of us want to enjoy mixed doubles with our spouses. However, also like the other couples we described, each of us has experienced that unfortunate on-court detonation that made us wonder if doing so was possible. Now, we are much better equipped to have an enjoyable time on the court. You can have a nice experience playing mixed doubles together. It's like your marriage: You have tools, and you work on it. By working together and using the tools, you'll craft a winning time together.

We have a mantra, "We play together, we win together, together we never lose." Make things happen on your and your spouse's terms.

Every now and then you may find yourself slipping into old behavior patterns. Don't be discouraged—hit your reset button and revisit the "Keys to Making it Work."

Stay committed to each other in your tennis approach. Empower each other to have fun and look forward to playing with one another. Enjoy your tennis journey; it can enrich your relationship.

We want to hear from you. Please visit our website at www.mixedtroubles.com. There's lots of good information to help you and your spouse enjoy mixed doubles. Please leave a comment or blog post.

Good luck!

Bibliography

Gallwey, Timothy W. <u>The Inner Game of Tennis</u>. New York: Random House, 1974,1977

Gray, John, Ph.D. <u>Men Are From Mars, Women Are From Venus</u>. New York: HarperCollins, 1992.

McEnroe, Patrick. <u>Tennis For Dummies</u>. Indianapolis: Wiley Publishing, 1998.

Osborne, Cecil G., D.D. <u>The Art of Understanding your Mate</u>. Grand Rapids: Zondervan Publishing House, 1970

Peck, M. Scott, M.D. <u>The Road Less Traveled</u>. New York: Simon & Schuster, 1978

Bibliography

Footnotes

1) "What is Mindset?' The Free Dictionary. www.thefreedictionary.com

2) <u>A Parents Guide: Teaching Tennis to Children Ten and Under.</u> USTA.com

3) <u>Testosterone, and winning and loosing in human competition</u>. Booth A., Shelly G., Mazur A., Tharp G., Kittok R. Hormones & Behavior. December 28, 1989

4) <u>The Battle of the Ms.</u> Vincent E. Faherty. MBA, DSW. Published online, October 25, 2008

5) The Sports Doc Chalk Talk. Dr. Chris Stankovich. September 25, 2013

6) <u>Handling Sports Pressure & Competition.</u> www.NBA.com. Reviewed by Darcy Lyness, PhD. October, 2010

7) Stressor. Definition of stressor. Dictionary.com

8) <u>Eustress vs. Distress</u>. Habits for Well-Being. www.habitsforwellbeing.com. June 29, 2017

9) Eustress. Wikipedia. en.wikipedia.org/wiki/Eustress

10) The prefix "eu". Wikipedia. En.wikipedia.org/wiki/eustress

11) Sports Psychology. Danielwarner1.blogsport.com. May 29, 2015

12) <u>Stepping Away From The Comfort Zone.</u> Joe Divosevic, Mac Gym. www.mymacgym.com

13) The Sports Doc Chalk Talk. Dr. Chris Stankovich. September 25, 2013

14) Communication defined. www.thefreedictionary.com

15) Character defined. www.thefreedictionary.com

16) <u>Playing Smart Doubles.</u> Tony Lance, tennismagazine.com. April 1, 2006

17) <u>Having Trouble Finding a Tennis Partner? Master These Five Skills and You'll Be the Most Sought-After Player at Your Club</u>. Manuela Davis, tennismagazine.com. April 17, 2006

18) <u>Tennis Strategy and Tactics.</u> People.ucls.uchicago.edu/-ghanck/htm/tactics/.html

ABOOKS

ALIVE Book Publishing and ALIVE Publishing Group
are imprints of Advanced Publishing LLC,
3200 A Danville Blvd., Suite 204, Alamo, California 94507

Telephone: 925.837.7303
alivebookpublishing.com

www.ingramcontent.com/pod-product-compliance
Lightning Source LLC
Chambersburg PA
CBHW031513270326
41930CB00006B/383